KNEE HIGH
BY THE
FOURTH OF JULY

*More Stories of Growing Up in and
Around Small Towns in the Midwest*

D1304348

Published by: Shapato Publishing
PO Box 476
Everly, IA 51338

ISBN: 978-0-9821058-7-0

Library of Congress Control Number: 2009909332
Copyright © 2009 Shapato Publishing

All rights reserved. No part of this book may be reproduced or transmitted in any form or by any means, electronic or mechanical, including photo-copying, recording, or by an information storage and retrieval system, without permission in writing from the publisher.

First Printing October 2009

Cover photo provided by Betty Hembd Taylor

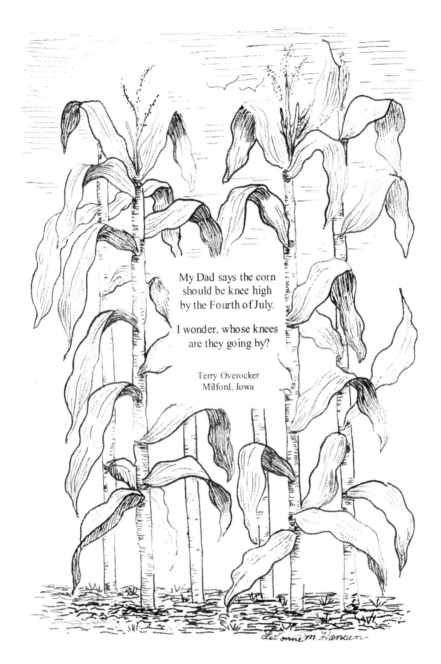

My Dad says the corn
should be knee high
by the Fourth of July.

I wonder, whose knees
are they going by?

Terry Overocker
Milford, Iowa

Drawing by LaVonne M. Hansen

Acknowledgements

Since the publication of *Walking Beans Wasn't Something You Did With Your Dog: Stories of Growing Up in and Around Small Towns in the Midwest*, in 2008, I've been honored to work with many talented authors.

Putting this book together has been a joy, but it has by no means been a solo effort.

First, I want to thank my husband, Grover Reiser, for being my partner in this business, as well as the most patient man in the world. There were many late nights and short tempers during this long, ongoing process, but he always made me feel that I could overcome any hurdle—and he's a good cook, besides.

Thank you to my children, Shaun Iske, Paul Iske and Toni Simon, for growing up to be fine adults despite my spotty parenting skills.

Thank you also to Orv Taylor of Hartley, Iowa, for catching a number of errors that would have slipped by this city girl, thus helping to ensure that this book is as good as it can be. Thank you, too, to Betty Taylor for being an excellent editor and, more than that, for being a truly good friend.

And thank you to our proofreaders—Sue, Deb and Ellen—for their hard work and sharp eyes. With their help this book is, I hope, as error-free as anything like this possibly can be, but if something has slipped through, I take full responsibility.

Jean Tennant
Everly, Iowa

Foreword

When Willa Cather wrote *O Pioneers!,* the first novel of her Nebraska trilogy, she found her voice, saying to her friend, "In this one I hit the home pasture." What makes her novel stand out is her attention to the details of that life and place. The novel begins on a bitter day in Hanover, a windswept town with a deep rutted main street. I still remember the details of that scene of Emil crying because his kitten climbed the telephone pole and had to be rescued by Carl. I can see Maria from Omaha in her red coat in the store. I can hear the rattle of the wagon and the howling wind as Alexandra and Emil head for home and their eyes spot "a rusty stovepipe sticking up through the sod" or "a windmill gaunt against the sky." Today I live in Sioux City and teach at Briar Cliff University. My days are spent indoors, not on the land, but it only takes a whiff of spring lilacs or the sound of wild turkeys outside my window or the sight of Indian grass on the hill above our campus to bring me back to those days on the farm or in the small towns of my childhood, Emmetsburg and Graettinger.

In this anthology, *Knee High by the Fourth of July,* many of these writers, like Willa Cather, hit the home pasture because their memories are vivid and rich.

Rebecca Groff describes making caramel corn for the Fourth of July but it was the detail of the navy blue and white speckled roaster pan that the popped corn was dumped into that sent my heart racing. As a child I used a similar blue speckled pan for emptying the popcorn and then adding butter. It was also the roaster mom used every Sunday to roast two of our chickens for dinner. Arlene Walker explains how it was to harvest the corn by hand in the days before we had corn pickers or combines. I don't remember that but I do recall how "Sometimes our clothes brushed against dried cocklebur plants. Prickly, clingy cockle-burs could be removed only by pulling them off one by one." When I'd go in search of pumpkins in late September, I'd feel my pant legs catch on the burrs and know I'd be picking those out one by one.

Verla Klaessy describes the dangers of getting lost in a corn field. "I was somewhat aware that if you stayed on the same row you would come to the end, eventually." I remember my own father warning me to not even go in there or "they'll find your bones in the fall." Betty Hembd Taylor writes, "Stones continue to work their way to the surface of the land and farmers continue to pick them up every spring." I'm reminded of Ted Kooser's poem "Abandoned Farmhouse" where the speaker says that the person who once lived there was "not a man for farming, says the field / cluttered with boulders." In my childhood picking up rock was a chore we seemed to do Good Friday morning—if the fields were dry enough.

Ruth Hunziker Underhill told me something I didn't know. "Silk stockings were scarce because the silk was used for parachutes. That's when skin creams made to cover the legs and look like stockings debuted." And I thought artificial tanning lotion was a somewhat new product. Marilyn Wells tells the story of delivering papers with the help of her horse and one morning it climbed up onto the neighbor's porch, leaving a deposit of road apples.

Vivian Eucker writes that her father-in-law Carl, who never received any training, was stationed in New Guinea. "The soldiers would bring him a pair of worn pants and he'd fashion a billed cap" to protect them from the sun.

Jane Kauzlarich writes of her pet crow eating little balls of bread dipped in milk, pecking caps off the milk bottles and scaring the wits out of a neighbor boy when it went after the metal studs on his jeans.

There are thirty-three writers in this anthology, and they leave me with many details and images that cover a period of 100 years or more. After I finished I could still see a girl watching a tornado, another woman holding kittens in the hayloft and crying because her husband was in Vietnam, a tree stump landing in a living room, an obsessed car-chasing dog, neighbors hiding a car so it couldn't be sold in farm foreclosure auction, hot casseroles brought to homes, Isinglass panels in the door of a stove, saved bacon drippings, blizzards (both black and white), red barns, a baseball glove landing in the tank beneath the privy, the embarrassment of wearing skunk shoes, using the wringer washer, and so many more.

It's the concrete details that trigger our memories. These stories from writers across the Midwest do just that. You will find yourself transported to that warm place where your memories have been stored. Enjoy the trek back as you read "remembrances of things past."

I know I did.

Tricia Currans-Sheehan teaches at Briar Cliff University and is editor of *The Briar Cliff Review*. She has had works published in *Connecticut Review*, *Crab Orchard Review*, *Virginia Quarterly Review*, *Fiction*, *The Long Story*, *Portland Review*, *Puerto del Sol*, *Calyx*, *Frontiers: A Journal of Women Studies*, *South Dakota Review*, *Kalliope*, *Wisconsin Review*, and many other journals. Her collection of short stories, *The Egg Lady and Other Neighbors* (November 2005), won The Headwaters Literary Competition sponsored by New Rivers Press. Her second book, *The River Road: A Novel in Stories*, was released in November 2008 from NRP. Visit www.currans-sheehan.com to learn more about her works.

Award-winning artist LaVonne M. Hansen lives in Hartley, Iowa. Her pen-and-ink drawings appear in the recent auto-biography, *Climbing—One Pole at a Time*, by Irvin Goodon, and the soon-to-be-published memoir, *The Earth Abides*, by Betty Hembd Taylor. Several of her drawings also appear in these pages.

CONTENTS

Photo provided by Betty Hembd Taylor

KNEE HIGH
BY THE
FOURTH OF JULY

*More Stories of Growing Up in and
Around Small Towns in the Midwest*

Edited by Jean Tennant

Shapato Publishing
Everly, Iowa

Photo provided by Arlene Walker

PICKING CORN EAR BY EAR

Arlene Walker

Colorful autumn days on our Iowa farm turned into chilly nights before a killing frost ended the growing season. Tall, tassel-topped rows of corn that had graced the fields near the farmplace all summer turned brown. Ears of corn covered with silk formed inside husks that had pointed skyward now hung heavy and mature, ready for harvest.

Our family experienced the corn season from start to finish. Early in the spring Dad used our faithful team of horses to spread manure over the field, which fertilized the ground. Then he disked the field before planting the corn.*

Weeks after planting, whenever we drove down country roads to church or to town, Dad commented about fields of sprouting corn. Looking out of the back window of the car, I was fascinated by the checked design of the cornfields, perfect rows in every direction, whizzing past the car window. When the corn was still a few inches high, Dad started cultivating. He cultivated the field a second and third time in opposite directions.

Around the fourth of July Dad walked into the field and measured the height of the growing stalks. We children followed him, but it was Dad's knees, not ours, that measured the growing corn. If the stalks were as tall as Dad's knees, he happily announced that the crop was on schedule. If any of us children dared go into the cornfield after it was taller than our heads, we knew we could get lost, so none of us ventured very far into the green jungle.

Harvesting the crop took the help of our whole family. Unpredictable weather changes from warm to cold, dry to rainy or sometimes snowy made it necessary to harvest the corn as quickly as possible before the first heavy snowfall. If all went well, harvesting could be completed before Thanksgiving.

Just as our farm had no electricity or running water, so the equipment used for picking corn was simple. Dad owned a wooden wagon with tall metal wheels and long wooden spokes that connected to a hub in the center. Before the corn picking, Dad equipped the wagon with a bang board fitted over its right side. The bang board made a target easier than trying to throw the picked ears directly into the wagon. Our team of gentle horses was hitched, and pulled the wagon by its long tongue.

The only other piece of equipment Dad used was a hook on a strap that he fastened around his wrist and the palm of his left hand over his glove. The hook was used to loosen the dried husk on the ear of corn. This speeded up the time it took to pick the ear with the free hand and toss it against the bang board so it would drop into the wagon. We children weren't equipped with hand hooks because it took skill to learn how to use them without getting hurt by the sharp ends. We were, however, supplied with orange flannel gloves that could be worn on either hand because of an extra thumb on the back side. When the palms of the gloves became worn with holes, the gloves could be turned over and put on opposite hands so the holes would be on top of the hand. The gloves were too large, but with practice I learned how to peel back the husks and bend the ears so they would break away, leaving the husk on the stalk.

Our family didn't harvest on Sunday, but we worked hard after school and on Saturdays. After Mom fed us a hot breakfast, she urged us to wear layers of warm clothing. As we crossed the yard to the field, we saw our breath in front of us. In the crisp, morning air, ears of corn hitting the bang board in rhythm and Dad's commands to the horses "Giddyap!" "Whoa!" "Back!" were a clear call for us to help.

My brother and I picked rows next to the wagon. Dad picked rows farther out. My younger sister knew how to husk ears, but she was not tall enough to aim at the bang board. Dad told her to pick from rows ahead of the wagon and pile the ears on the ground. Dad praised her speed as he picked up each pile of ears. She didn't tire of the game and went about it cheerfully.

There were times when I wanted to sneak away between the tall, rustling stalks where now and then a rabbit appeared and sped into hiding, or a startled pheasant squawked suddenly before it flew away. But fearful thoughts of getting lost, along with a sense of dedication to the task at hand, kept me picking ear after ear.

Whenever we complained, Dad encouraged us: "Our wagon is almost full!" or "We're almost done with these rows, then we'll go in the house for supper."

Mom helped some with the picking, but she also prepared our meals, leaving them to simmer on the back of the cookstove. Then she did the chores, gathering the eggs and milking the cows.

On cold days the ground was firm, but our hands and feet became easily chilled. Picking fast helped keep us warm. On days after it had rained or the snow melted, mud clung to the bottom of shoes or boots, the added weight making it more difficult to walk. We laughed at the elevated soles of our shoes made by the clinging mud. The horses had to work extra hard to pull a load of corn over wet ground.

Sometimes our clothes brushed against dried cocklebur plants. Prickly, clingy cockleburs could be removed only by pulling them off one by one.

On good days we filled one to two wagonloads, each load about forty bushels. Dad shoveled the corn from the wagon into the corncrib. When that became full, he rigged up makeshift cribs using woven wire or snow fence. It was important that the corn be dry before storing because wet corn turned black with mold after time and could no longer be used for feeding pigs and cattle.

As the autumn sun set and darkness made it impossible to see in the field, we dragged our weary bodies across the farm-yard to the house. Warm, inviting supper smells greeted us, as did the cozy fire in the cookstove. After supper Mom brought out Corn Huskers Lotion for our hands, which were chapped from the cold and from handling the rough ears of corn.

It was a goal to finish corn harvest by Thanksgiving. After that the threat of heavy snow loomed. Completing harvest was marked by a simple celebration with hot chocolate around a crackling fire.

Changes in time brought about more sophisticated methods of planting and harvesting corn. The task of husking corn by hand instilled in farm children a strong work ethic. The memories of a simple, hardworking lifestyle were not forgotten.

*A roll of wire with buttons attached every 40 inches was fastened to stakes and pushed into the ground at both ends of the row. The corn planter was equipped with two planter boxes that held corn. When the planter was pulled by our team of horses, the buttons in the wire tripped a device on the corn boxes so three kernels of corn were dropped and planted every forty inches.

Arlene Walker, a retired teacher, was raised on a farm in northwest Iowa. She enjoys reading, cooking, quilting, walking, and writing personal experiences and stories for children.

Photo provided by Verla Klaessy

A CORNFIELD JUNGLE

Verla Klaessy

"Come on, I know the way." As an adventurous four-year-old I was coaxing my cousin, who was my age, to follow me down the row of tall cornstalks that rustled in the breeze and towered over our heads.

I lived on the farm with my parents. Marjean, my cousin who resided in town, often came to visit. In the late August sun on this day we had played happily in the yard for a while. When we tired of the sandpile we played on the swing hanging from the huge mulberry tree and chased butterflies.

Marjean had come to the farm with our grandmother who was busy peeling and slicing apples along with my mother and another aunt, and putting many quarts in glass jars for use in the winter.

As we wandered out of the fenced yard and headed for the sheep barn, Marjean hung back. She was apprehensive about farm animals. But the sheep had kind faces and weren't as scary as the big cows or grunting pigs.

After petting a couple of sheep, I led the way toward the big red barn. The bottom half of the side door opened easily and there was a big pile of sweet-smelling hay to jump into. We laughed and giggled, the sound echoing to the haymow. A startled kitten jumped out from behind a feed trough and raced to the back of the barn. Our laughter continued as we ran after the soft bundle of fur. We caught it and held it for a moment, then the chase was on again.

Through the back door we saw lazy clouds floating in the azure sky. The sun was warm and the adjoining cornfield beckoned to us. Our legs were short, but we managed to scale a low wooden fence. As we skipped across a field lane, I kept urging my companion forward.

Grandpa, our uncle and my daddy were digging potatoes in a field just beyond the cornfield.

"Let's go find Grandpa. We can help dig potatoes," I persuaded. Every once in a while we could hear the men's voices waft across the breeze.

Bravely, I grabbed my cousin's hand and pulled her into the cornfield. We were immediately hidden from any outsider's view.

In the meantime, we were missed at the house. The three women ran out onto the porch, calling our names. They searched the yard. One headed for the grove, another searched the garage and washhouse. The third headed for the corncrib. Then they congregated at the barn, calling, shouting and pleading for an answer. They were frantic. Fearfully they checked the water tank, the haymow, the pasture where the cows and horses were kept, the sheep barn and the hog lot.

Panic had set in. How could two little tots completely disappear?

In the rows of corn, the gentle breeze blew through the top of the green stalks. The dirt path was wide enough for two sets of tiny slippers padding down the row. Looking ahead and looking behind were the same continuous green plants with ears of corn hanging from them. I was somewhat aware that if you stayed on the same row you would come to the end, eventually. As we were traveling the width of the field instead of the length, we came to the edge of the small field in less than a quarter of an hour.

In the distance we saw the men busy with the potato harvest. The men stopped their work, amazed to see two little girls emerging from the nearby field. We ran breathlessly into their arms, saying proudly, "We s'prised you!"

We didn't notice the relieved looks the men exchanged. Then they took us by our hands. Grandpa led us to his big black Model-T Ford coupe and drove with us back to the neighboring farm.

We didn't understand all the commotion upon our return. The women, gathered by the gate, greeted us with tears and cries of joy.

After quick hugs and explanations, I was feeling quite proud that I'd found the way and pulled off a big surprise. Pride was short-lived, however. My mother pulled me aside, gave me a severe paddling and sent me to bed for the rest of the afternoon.

Grandmother cuddled Marjean in her arms. My cousin was not even scolded, because it had really been all *my* fault!

Such was the end of our adventurous episode in the cornfield jungle.

Verla Klaessy of Spencer, Iowa, has traveled in all fifty states, Canada, Mexico, and Europe. She worked in the Spencer Elementary Schools as librarian for 16 years. Since her retirement she has been writing extensively, with her poetry appearing in *Lyrical Iowa*.

Carmel Corn

Original recipe of Gertrude Theresa Zobel

1/2 - 10-ounce can popcorn
2 cups Br. sugar
3 tablespoons corn syrup
1/2 cup butter
Pinch of baking soda

Method: First pop corn.

Then cook the sugar, syrup and butter in lg pan, stirring constantly, until a few drops of syrup tested in cold water feel brittle.

Remove from heat, stir in soda and pour over corn.

THE TIME OF SNAKES
AND SPARKLERS AND CARMEL CORN

Rebecca Groff

My father's most memorable Fourth of July revolved around fifteen cents. Obtaining enough daily food and decent clothing were constant challenges for him, his twin sister and his divorced mother, let alone having real money in hand throughout the Depression years. But one Fourth of July when he and sister Eleanor were nine years old my grandmother gave each of them three nickels. Dad spent one nickel on an ice cream cone, another nickel on a carnival ride and the last nickel on a pack of firecrackers. That was the sum total of his Fourth of July celebration that summer, and he considered himself lucky to have that.

For me, the memories of past Fourths are more fortunate, and at the center of these recollections is one key item—caramel corn. I share the exact spelling of the word *carmel* here with you as it's written in my mother's faded blue-inked handwriting on a yellowed and tattered three-by-four inch index card from her tin recipe box. That precious collection of well-used recipe cards resides in Michigan with my sister these days. While our mother was a fine speller, she did write the word as c-a-r-m-e-l, the reason for which rests with her now, and remains unknown to us.

Every year on the afternoon of the Fourth my mother commenced caramel corn production.

She popped the corn in a heavy black cast-iron frying pan on top of an electric range. She'd pour a small circle of Crisco oil into the bottom of the pan before depositing a small measure of dull gold kernels. Then, holding a lid in place over the pan to keep the exploding kernels from escaping, she'd scrape and *scooch* the pan back and forth rapidly across the top of the burner to keep the kernels moving so they wouldn't scorch before they had time to heat, expand—and *pop!* The panful of popped corn was then dumped into a navy blue and white speckled roaster pan to wait for the next critical step.

Brown sugar, butter and Karo syrup came together in an aqua-colored aluminum pan my mother dubbed the "candy pan." Once the boiled tan mixture was ready she added soda and poured it over the mound of popcorn, stirring to coat things evenly. Small samplings were necessary to be sure the batches *passed muster*, a favorite expression of my mother's. And they always did.

At dusk we'd transport the butterscotch-colored delight in a brown paper grocery sack to Cemetery Road, a graveled path out in the country a few miles from our house. Cemetery Road bordered the final resting spots of many of the town's former residents. It made for perfect viewing of the fireworks display the Chamber of Commerce volunteers fired off once nightfall set in. We never waited for the sky to light up with exploding spraying colors before diving into The Best Caramel Corn in the World. What better way to pass time than munching sticky handfuls of caramel corn as we waited for the show to begin! Sometimes we'd strike gold, pulling out a large cluster with an extra thick coating.

It wasn't a Fourth of July without firecrackers, and while they weren't exactly legal in the state of Iowa at the time, we'd hear them going off all day long around town. It seemed only fitting that they did, but not everyone shared this view. One year our mayor caused quite a stir among the teen arena by banning the presence of all firecrackers within city limits. We heard them popping and snapping around town anyway.

I know my brothers participated in their fair share of the somewhat-illicit black cats, cherry bombs and pop-bottle rockets. My sister and I, however, were content with the less dangerous types of fireworks, such as the curious black tablets we could buy at that time. We'd place the small round charcoal pieces on the sidewalk, light them with a match, and then stand back and watch as ominous, spiraling, grayish-black cinder snakes grew up from the paving—leaving stains that required several cleansing rains to remove.

My personal favorite firecrackers were the tiny colored balls we'd toss hard against the sidewalk, anticipating their high-pitched *snap!* We felt cheated when we'd get a dud that wouldn't explode. Their colors—raspberry pink, turquoise blue, bright orange and yellow—reminded me of the larger, edible jaw-breaker candies we'd buy at the Five-and-Dime store. I was hugely irritated when these little poppers were no longer for sale in the stores, having gone the way of "dangerous and harmful," not to mention illegal.

Some years our town hosted large horse shows, during which equine competitors traveled from surrounding states to show off their high-dressed Arabian beauties and compete for tall gold trophies in our city park. One year my sister and I were chosen to present trophies to the winners. It should have been an honor, and in a way it was, but I also remember it being a drawn-out, sticky job that scorching Iowa July afternoon, and we were both glad when it was over.

Other years the local Chamber of Commerce organized watermelon-eating contests, baseball games and various foot races for children in the city park. Once I entered a three-legged-race, placed, and won fifty cents. Cradling that shiny half-dollar piece in my hand, I felt like the richest kid in the world. Not wanting to lose the feeling, I put the coin in a treasure box in my bedroom and took it out every now and then to hold. I suppose I eventually spent it on taffies or jawbreakers at the local Five-and-Dime, but I savored the time it was in my possession.

We always ended the Fourth of July by lighting sparklers. My Dad had no interest in them and would go to bed. But my mother, my sister and youngest brother, along with his best friend, and I would move to our backyard with a generous supply of sparklers, stick matches and the essential empty Folgers coffee can in which to place our burned rods. A corn field backed up to our yard, so we'd each light a sparkler and take off running between the rows of corn that were definitely taller than knee-high, but far from the full height they would reach by late summer.

"Knee-high corn by the Fourth" has become a casual myth, but long-ago farmers used it to gauge whether they'd planted their corn in ample time that spring, and had hopes for warm weather and decent moisture to ensure a good crop. Corn matures differently under different conditions, and that old saying was little more than a vague rule of thumb. But I heard my dad say it many times as we drove past early fields. He'd gradually decelerate the car as he studied the young corn intently, smiling and saying, "The farmers are going to have a good year."

Healthy corn always made my dad smile. A good year for the farmers meant a good year for his welding repair business.

With our sparklers lit, we'd run along the young rows of corn, and I always had this fear of encountering a raccoon in the cornfield. Raccoons like corn, but as it was early in the growing season no ears had come on yet and my fears never materialized.

With our coffee tin full of spent matches and burned, curled sparkler rods, our Fourth of July came to an end, and we headed to bed knowing we'd done justice to the holiday.

When the Fourth of July rolls around these days I get an empty feeling if I haven't heard any firecrackers. It doesn't seem like a proper red-white-and-blue celebration until I hear at least a few of the signature pops and explosions that I remember so well from my childhood.

Every year now my husband and I host an annual Fourth of July barbecue in our yard. We don't light sparklers or shoot off firecrackers, but we enjoy the lively camaraderie of close friends and neighbors along with tables full of grilled meats, baked beans, fresh summer fruits and homemade pies as we wait for nightfall. With folding chairs and drinks in tow we wander down to the empty field at the edge of our neighborhood where we watch someone else's fireworks across a dusky sky. Last year I made buttered popcorn for our guests to take along. An empty bowl at the end of the evening suggested my choice had been a winner. Maybe next year I'll make caramel corn.

Freelance writer **Rebecca Groff** lives in Cedar Rapids, Iowa. Her work has been published in regional as well as national magazines, anthologies and online literary web sites. She is hunting for a publisher for her novel *Iron Angel*, while continuing to produce new work.

Drawing by LaVonne M. Hansen   The Hembd Farmstead, circa 1942

A HARVEST OF STONES

Haibun*

Betty Hembd Taylor

wonders of childhood
stones in flowing creek waters
splashes of joy

I spent many childhood hours playing in the grove behind the barn with my sister and brother. But at times I sought to escape them and played alone on the large fieldstones in the stream running through that grove. I sailed the seven seas on those stones or rafted down the river with Tom and Huck. Sometimes I delivered orations to livestock as they looked at me quizzically while they wandered among the trees or drank from the creek. I imagined a thousand plays atop my stone stage and acted them out with imaginary friends. Through ensuing years, the size of the stones grew ever larger in my fantasies, fitting with the importance they played in my childhood.

Around the year 1900, the first owners of my parents' farm gathered fieldstones for the foundations of buildings on their farmstead. Skilled stonemasons set the unevenly shaped boulders in place for substantial footings and substructure. Later, from the early forties until the late sixties, three generations of Hembds picked up rocks from the fields just to get them out of the way.

As I matured, stones continued to intrigue me. Glacial history, the evidence of their use for tools, and the sturdy structures blending with the countryside are subjects I find to be of unending interest.

Settlers in various parts of the country chose farmland for many reasons. Some might have loved rolling hills, which reminded them of previous European homes, or wooded lands with plentiful trees for building and fuel. Others purposely chose areas with rocks, which provided materials for foundations or fences, and in some instances, whole structures.

On Highway 18, just outside Hartley, Iowa, stands an attractive example of a fieldstone house. In 1932, Arnold and Catherine Albrecht had it built as a place to raise their small children. Unfortunately, Arnold's life was short. Without him, Catherine, whose character was as sturdy as the stones that formed her house, tenaciously hung on to the place. She managed and paid for the farm, raised her children, and sent them all to college. I became acquainted with Arnold's brother, Raymond, in the 1970s. He had retired from being a full-time pastor and moved to Hartley, serving as a part-time pastor who ministered to shut-ins for St. Paul's Lutheran Church. Once he told me that he had helped with the tedious task of gathering the stones for that landmark house.

The value of using fieldstones for building is also evident along the shores of Lake Okoboji in Northwest Iowa. There one sees stone fences, foundations, and entire rustic buildings. The shore patrol station and lodge at Gull Point State Park on West Lake Okoboji are excellent examples of stone masonry. Civilian Conservation Corps workers, using rounded colorful rocks and boulders, built them in the late 1930s.

Stones continue to work their way to the surface of the land, and farmers continue to pick them up every spring, to keep them from harming machinery. They find the stony fields to be more frustrating than charming.

Stonemasons are now in short supply. Straighter man-made materials, which are more easily stacked and mortared, are preferred for building. In the early 1940s my father arranged to have a new foundation laid under the barn when the original fell into disrepair. I don't recall what he did with the majority of the rocks and boulders. Perhaps, as do the current owners of the place, he hired someone to bury them. But I well recall the time, when with the help of neighbors, he loaded some of the remnants of the old foundation onto horse-pulled *stone boats*, hauled them to the grove, and deposited them into the stream. I shared my parents' pride in the neat rows of the new cement block foundation, but most of all, I relished having rocks to enhance my playground.

shrouded truths surface
ground and smoothed by time's passage
my heart's stony soil.

On a June day in 1984, I received the opportunity to revisit my memorable childhood haunts. At a family reunion, one of my nieces announced that the current owners of the farm were going to burn the old house to make room for a newer one, which would be moved onto the place. They extended an invitation for us to tour it before that fateful day. Not only had the house been our family home, but it had also been home to each of my three brothers and their families at different times. Two generations of us had fond memories of the place, and we wanted to share those memories with a third.

One nephew helped me glean squares of Victorian corners from woodwork around windows and doors. We also took grates from around stovepipe holes. I recounted evenings when we crept from our beds, lay on the floor around those grates, and listened to adult conversations below. Nieces and nephews confessed to doing the same thing in later times.

In honor of our mother's memory we posed for a picture in front of the double living room windows. She often lined us up there for pictures during World War II, so the service flags, representing family members in the Army, Air Force and WAVES would be in the finished photos. One sister was absent that day, but three of the four remaining siblings lined up for one last picture on that memorable spot.

After much reminiscing, along with pensive thoughts, laughter, and good-natured accusations, I encouraged nieces and nephews to come to the grove with me. I wanted them to see the magical place where I once played, and experience the magnificent rocks in the stream.

But a startling sight awaited me. The rocks and boulders had settled deeply into the creek bottom during the years since I played there. Yet, I was forced to realize they never could have been as large as the fantasy.

I was still recovering from the shock of how small they actually were, when one of my nephews clarified what I was seeing. As he pointed things out to his son, I heard him say, "Look. Those were Aunt Betty's stepping stones."

The house was burned soon after that indelible visit, and the barn met a similar fate at a later time. A more modern house and barn occupy their places now. I am pleased that the buildings have not been allowed to deteriorate and fall apart, as is a common sight in rural Midwest. Parts of the grove remain, and more trees have been added. It is comforting to see that the site has not been plowed and planted.

I recognize familiar lines of some of the smaller well-kept buildings, and see that some earth moving and landscaping have made the renovation complete. A swing set stands on the lawn. Among the many changes and improvements, I observe that the area Dad called "permanent pasture" raises row-crops now.

My memories, too, have changed and evolved with the passing of time. Few things remain constant in our lives, but the stream continues to run and a stony harvest continues to rise to the surface, offering ongoing challenges every spring.

> *memories of childhood*
> *like stones settling in creek beds*
> *eroded, refined*

*Haibun was originally a Japanese form of writing, a combination of prose and haiku poetry. Haiku, a form of poetry with seventeen or fewer syllables, is an insight into a moment of experience, and a haibun is the story or narrative of how one came to have that experience.

Betty Hembd Taylor's roots reach deeply into the rich but stony soil of the Midwest. She and her husband live in Hartley, Iowa. Her work has appeared in *Walking Beans Wasn't Something You Did With Your Dog, Lyrical Iowa, Julien's Journal, Capper's* and *The Hartley Sentinel.* She is in the process of formatting a collection of her own poems and essays for the soon-to-be-released, *The Earth Abides.*

Drawing by LaVonne M. Hansen

The Albrecht House

Photo provided by Vivian Eucker

UNTRAINED VALOR

Vivian Eucker

It seems inconceivable that the Army would send any young man into war without training. Participants in D-Day during World War II received training. Even replacement forces needed later in the war received a fast basic training of nine to twelve weeks. But my father-in-law, Carl A. Eucker, is an unassuming man who has been reluctant to share his service story. He's written the chronological data of his tour of duty in the family history. His heirs and others deserve to know the full story of this humble man's untrained valor.

Carl Eucker was inducted on December 29, 1941, and sent to Leavenworth, Kansas, where he received his uniform. From there, his group went to Texas. The men were asked which field they wanted to work in, and Carl signed up for mechanic's training. He was then put on a list to go to Fort Dix, New Jersey, and Carl's unit joined another outfit. From Fort Dix the group was sent to New York City Harbor and put on a ship to go overseas. All of this took only two weeks' time. Due to his group being attached to the 403 Heavy-Bomb group, he missed basic training.

Carl's ship joined a convoy from the west coast that was traveling to Melbourne, Australia. The trip took about a month. In order to prevent the enemy from seeing the movement of the troops, the convoy was ordered to maintain a blackout. This meant that not only were the lights on the top of the ship off, but the portholes were also closed and covered. No fresh air circulated within the troop carrier.

"It took us a month to get to Melbourne, and most of the guys got seasick. It was a mess," said Carl.

Carl Eucker's unit worked with the Australians for three months. While there, he learned to pack parachutes and take care of the emergency equipment, mainly the life rafts and vests. He also trained to equip the emergency rations for the parachutes. While he was learning this from the Australians, his fellow soldiers were doing some basics and KP. Carl smiles when he recounts that he never had to do KP.

By October 17, 1942, Carl Eucker was stationed at Iron Range, in Australia. He then traveled to New Guinea, being stationed at Melne Bay, Port Moresby, and Dobodura.

"On January 17, 1943, the enemy gave a daylight raid and destroyed three of the B-17 planes in the runway," said Carl. "It was close enough we lost everything in our tents and there were four guys in a twelve-by-twelve tent. Luckily, no lives were lost. Since I was always with the supply guys, I saw the air strike. The bombs didn't go into the ground, but exploded on top and did more damage. Besides the planes, a tractor was upset and destroyed." My father-in-law believed this was one of the most frightening times during his service.

After this incident, the men were jumpy. Carl remembers one night when the troops were watching a movie. The movie house of Dobodura, New Guinea was like a drive-in, with a large screen hung on an enormous pole frame. The projection box was similar to the crow's nest from which the football games were announced at Newman Grove's football field in Nebraska, near where Carl had lived. The projectionist had to climb a ladder to start the reels.

Carl and his tentmates were wisely perched upon a nearby hill to watch the film. Suddenly, something flashed across the screen. It might have been a bird, or even a flaw in the film, but the fact that no one knew *what* it was made it frightening. An unknown shadow flitting momentarily across the screen scared the men into a stampede similar to a herd of cattle being frightened by a coyote. Some men were injured in the crush. Carl and a few others were lucky to be on the hillside.

Parachute-packing might have been an easier job back in the states, but in Australia, where Carl learned how to pack a parachute, there were open-air hangers and tables. Carl remembers there being an office also. This is where he did all of his packing of parachutes. By the time he arrived at New Guinea, all the men who went up in planes were responsible for their own chutes. Carl does remember that the parachute packs needed rations. These rations, particularly the candy bars, frequently disappeared. Though Carl suspected the pilots, he never knew for certain who was doing the snitching. Once the candy bars were gone, there was nothing to replenish the supply. It was at this time that Carl began taking responsibility for the life rafts on each plane. When a plane would return, Carl had to test the life rafts by inflating, deflating, and refolding them. These life rafts were crucial to a pilot downed over the water.

Never one to be idle, Carl Eucker kept busy even after duty. With a sewing machine he acquired in Australia, he sewed caps out of used pants. The soldiers would bring him a pair of worn-out pants, and he would fashion a billed cap. The Army distributed hats, but they didn't protect the men from the sun and climate of New Guinea. Being a farmer from Nebraska, Carl knew exactly what was needed. He made functional caps for the men, earning several hundred dollars during his tour. He sent this money home to his family in Nebraska.

Even though the Army didn't give Carl Eucker basic training, I believe my father-in-law was in training for his tour of duty all his life. Carl's mother died when he was twelve. This forced him into adulthood at an early age. He wasn't homesick during his service years as many young soldiers were, because at the age of sixteen he traveled to Iowa in a Model-A Ford. In Iowa he shucked grain and eventually joined a threshing crew.

The second year he hitchhiked to Minnesota to thresh. He spent three or four summers working away from home, then, back in Nebraska, farmed before he entered the service. The Midwest work ethic and values were the training that led to his heroism on a fateful day.

Frank Farquhar, a friend of Carl's who was a pilot, needed to make a test run of one of the B-17 planes. He asked Carl and several others if they'd like to go up in the plane. The men piled in. But, as the plane began to lift off, something went wrong. The plane sputtered and crashed at the end of the runway.

Frank Farquhar was injured and trapped in the cockpit. He yelled for help as the other men ran from the wreckage, fearful of an explosion. Carl stopped and went back to the cockpit. He pulled Frank from the plane.

The plane exploded just seconds after Carl and Frank made their escape. Frank never forgot this act of valor on Carl's part.

It's inconceivable that the Army would send any young man into war without training. Carl Eucker was issued a gun but never trained in how to use it to defend himself or others. He was sent into war only with Australian training in how to pack a parachute. Yet without basic training, Carl Eucker attained the highest rank a non-commissioned officer could receive, going from private to technical sergeant.

The lessons of life led Carl to save a man from the burning wreckage of a plane. This unassuming, humble man may have been untrained by the Army, but remains a man of valor in the eyes of his family.

Vivian Eucker is the daughter-in-law of Carl Eucker and an English teacher at Newman Grove Public Schools. She and her husband, Carmen, live near Albion, Nebraska, on the farm established by Carl and Elaine Eucker. They have three children: Tracy Jarosik, Jeffrey Eucker, and Amber Salwei.

Photo provided by Ruth Hunziker Underhill

SUGAR RATIONING
AND CHRISTMAS COOKIES

Ruth Hunziker Underhill

I was only eight years old when President Franklin D. Roosevelt declared that the United States was at war. At that time it wasn't significant to me, but as the years went on and life at home was affected by the war, it began to take on a more sober meaning.

My mother had five brothers who all served in World War II at the same time. During that war, the government gave a banner with a blue star on a red and white background to the families who had children or spouses serving our country. My grandmother had five blue stars displayed in the window of her home for several years.

For our vacation each summer, my sisters and I got to stay, two at a time, at Grandma's house for two weeks in the summer.

Grandma would gather up a basket of clothes and take it out into the front yard under a big shade tree to do her weekly darning. For those of you who don't know what darning is, it's repairing and mending holes in socks and clothing. . . something that is rarely done today. My sisters and I would scamper around the yard playing games while she sat under the tree. Many times as she was sitting there diligently doing her darning, I saw that her cheeks were wet with tears. I always wondered why she was crying. Years later, I knew. I can only imagine the pain and heartache that she must have felt at having five sons on foreign lands fighting for our freedom, not knowing if she would ever see any of them again.

I'm sure the tears included prayers offered up on behalf of her beloved sons. God did answer those prayers, for all five of her sons returned home safe and sound from the war.

During that time of war, everything possible in our country had to be used for our troops and for ammunition. Many women began working in factories across our nation to replace the men who were drafted into the service. I remember my two aunts walking up Grandma's long lane each afternoon to catch a ride to the factory where they worked on the night shift.

As a result of so many commodities being needed for the war, a rationing program was enacted by our government. Each person was issued coupon booklets for many different items. Things rationed were silk stockings, shoes, rubber tires, gas, sugar and probably many more that I don't remember.

The shoe coupons we girls were issued were often used for our older brothers, who needed shoes worse than we did because they worked the fields and outgrew their shoes faster.

Silk stockings were scarce because the silk was used for parachutes. That's when skin creams made to cover the legs and look like stockings debuted. If ever real silk stockings were available, women flocked to the stores to snatch them up.

Dad was always concerned as to whether he'd have enough tire and gas coupons for the family. Butter was scarce, too, even on the farm. That's when the substitute oleo came on stage. When it first was introduced it came in a small plastic bag, one-pound size, and it was white. It looked like lard. A little capsule of yellow food coloring was included that you were supposed to squeeze and knead into it to give the yellow color of butter. Dad always said that oleo was an insult to the cows!

The sugar Mom used in her cooking had to be watched very carefully to make it last until the next coupon book was issued.

One summer day Mom said, "I don't think we are going to be able to bake any Christmas cookies this year. I just don't think I'll be able to make the sugar reach to include that."

A traditionalist at heart, I almost panicked at Mom's announcement. The thought of not being able to bake Christmas cookies was more than my little girl's heart could comprehend. Even though I was only about ten years old at the time, I kept thinking, "There's just gotta be a way around this!"

So one day, when no one else was around, I made a trip down to the cellar and very inconspicuously brought up a big gallon glass jar, washed it out, took it up to our walk-in attic and hid it under some blankets. From then on, once a week when no one else was around, I took a cup of sugar out of Mom's canister, traipsed up to the attic and dumped it into my treasured glass jar. When the jar was full I got another one and repeated my secret activity.

About two weeks before Christmas Mom once again lamented that she sure wished she could stretch the sugar so we could bake some Christmas cookies.

That was my great opportunity! I dashed upstairs, took a big glass jar in each hand, hurried down stairs and thrust them in front of Mom. Grinning, I said, "Will this be enough?"

Mom was flabbergasted. She lifted her head back and with wide eyes asked, "*Where* in the world did you get that?"

I revealed to her my childish scheme.

She said, "I thought my sugar was going down awfully fast!"

It worked. . . we got to bake Christmas cookies after all and they tasted better than any ever had before!

Ruth Hunziker Underhill was born on a farm in rural Eureka, Illinois. She graduated from Washington Community High School, Washington, Illinois, in 1951. She and her husband, Stephen, have been married for fifty-six years and have a daughter, Vickee, in Iowa, and a son, Todd, in Michigan. She has seven grandchildren and two great-grandchildren.

Photo provided by Marie Taylor Wells

SOLD OUT

Marie Taylor Wells

In the fall of 1930 when I was five and a half years old, a pall fell over our usually tranquil lives in a rambling farmhouse near Dickens, Iowa.

One night while I was playing quietly, I overheard Mother and Dad talking in hushed tones about being sold out. Though I didn't understand, I was frightened.

"Mom, what's 'sold out' mean? I asked fearfully the next day while she was kneading bread dough for our family of eight.

Mother looked startled. "It's nothing for you to worry your little head about," she said kindly.

If there was nothing to worry about, I wondered why they were so upset last night.

Years later, I learned that the Great Depression had settled over Middle America like the aftermath of a gigantic dust storm. The stock market that crashed the previous year, had gained and then struck bottom. Across the country, jobs were lost, businesses failed and prices for farm produce plummeted.

That was my father's dilemma that fall. After harvest, not enough money was generated from the farm products to pay off his bank loans for farm rent and other expenses. Soon the terrible day came when the banker sued Dad for delinquent payments.

Shortly after that, Dad was called into court where the judge ruled that the lawsuit was justified and ordered that his foreclosure, or selling out, was to be executed by March 1. Selling out meant the loss of Dad's animals and the implements essential for farming. It meant the loss of his livelihood, the only one he had known—one whose skills he had spent many years of his boyhood and manhood acquiring.

After supper that night, Dad and Mother told us that there would have to be an auction to sell all of the animals and machinery so that the loans at the bank could be paid. And we would have to move. We were stunned!

"Sell the horses?" "And the machinery?" "How could we farm?" "And move?" "Where would we move?" we asked. Our parents had no answers.

"Will we have to sell my car?" asked seventeen-year-old Howard, thinking of his rattle-trap coupe with the rumble seat.

"If you keep it at Grandma's in town," replied Dad, "they can't take it."

"Do we have to sell my kitties?" I cried to my sister Mildred as we climbed upstairs to bed. Mildred knew everything, I thought. She was twelve, and already a freshman in high school. When assured that they would be safe, I felt better. The kittens were precious to me. While my brothers were in school I would cuddle them and tell them all my problems.

Dad seemed to age years that day. Worry plowed deep furrows across his forehead. What if he couldn't farm? During the depression other jobs were nonexistent. He took such pride in providing for his family.

On the following snowy Saturday, a burly neighbor flagged down our ancient Dodge car as it passed his driveway. All eight of us, the back seat piled two deep, were on our way home from Dickens.

"Bob," shouted Mr. Swark, out of breath, "the sheriff's over at your place attaching everything. Better leave your car here so he can't list that too."

"Thanks," said Dad, shakily. "I really appreciate this." After the rest of us piled out, Dad drove into the neighbor's shabby protective shed. We all trudged through deepening snow down the road and up the lengthy driveway to our home. The sheriff had already departed. Everything we owned, with the exception of the household goods, was on the attachment list, thus, legally secured until the sale. Even the produce from the animals was no longer ours.

From then on, a deputy sheriff came twice a day to feed the livestock, milk the cows and gather the eggs. His attempts at milking caused a great deal of amusement among my brothers, who had learned to milk at age six.

"Old Roan just kicked the daylights out of him!" chortled ten-year-old Dale. "He's all covered with milk and manure." The next day the deputy informed Dad that we could keep the milk from Old Roan. It was a priceless commodity.

Fear and apprehension consumed all of us during the ensuing days. Dad was gone frequently, searching for another place to rent and to live. Mother tried to be cheerful, but looked very troubled.

"Mom, why do we have to sell Pet and the cows?" I wailed.

Mother could only shake her head and reply sorrowfully, "That's just the way it is."

So I stopped asking.

The afternoon before the sale, I pulled on my frayed coat, woolen tam and overshoes and followed my brothers down the path to the barn. I needed to say goodbye to the animals. Each cow was in her own stanchion eating her evening meal. Each seemed to bow politely as she dipped her head for more grain. I patted each one's head and called her by name as I told them goodbye.

When I ran over to the horse stalls, our eight gallant steeds stood munching great mouthfuls of hay while blowing huge billows of steam from their nostrils. They did not know that they would be sold the very next day. Would their masters be generous with food? Would they be kind?

With teary eyes I hugged Pet's small nose. "Goodbye, Pet," I sobbed. She was our red pony who stood stock still whenever I slipped off of her bare back. "Goodbye, Flory," I told our brown part-bronco. She was really fast and feisty. Only my two oldest brothers dared to ride her. Our other pairs were work horses. Prince and Lucy, our bright bays, were so gentle that Orville and Glen, ages seven and eight, could stand upright on their broad backs. After lavishing those horses with love, I passed quietly by Dick and Jim, red with black tails and manes, because Dick was blind and highly nervous. I bade farewell to the last pair, frisky Nig and big Dan, from a distance. They were huge and very scary.

Chilled, I hurried out of the barn past the array of worn farm machinery lined up as for a parade. Beside the two-bottom plow stood the corn planter with lidded boxes for seed. The cultivator used for digging up weeds was next to high-sided, wooden-wheeled wagons used for hand picking corn. Beyond that was the haying equipment. All power was furnished by the horses and men.

49

That night, knowing my dread of moving, Mother asked, "Marie, would you like to go to school when we move?"

"School? Oh, yes!" I exclaimed joyfully. "Could I?"

"We'll have to ask the teacher when we get there," replied Mom.

How I had longed to go to school, ever since Orville had gone almost two years before. Even though I was past five last fall, my parents decided I was too small to brave the cold and snow of the near-mile walk to the one-room schoolhouse. Dad always teased that I was just about knee-high to a grasshopper. Now that spring was near, they thought I could manage. March first was the legal farm moving day in Iowa, so teachers accepted transfer students then. But as I had never been in school, my parents needed to inquire if I too could be admitted.

The February sale day was clear and bone-chillingly cold when Mother woke us. We had no heat in our upstairs bedroom other than the bare wisps of warmth from the stove pipe rising from the log-fed metal stove in the living room below.

"It's too early," I protested as Mildred pried me out of my warm cocoon of blankets. She had already lighted the old kerosene lamp and had dressed herself. I scrambled out of my one-piece sleepers. With her help, we pulled on my icy long-legged underwear and long stockings. Whenever I could get away with it, I slept with the underwear under my sleepers, but with her overseeing me, that seldom happened.

"I'm so cold!" I shivered.

"Hurry up then," she commanded. "It's sale day. Dad wants to have an early breakfast."

I finished dressing and tugged on my high-top shoes which Mildred fastened with the button hook.

The delicious aroma of roast beef hash drew us downstairs. Since we didn't eat between meals, Mother prepared protein-laden healthful foods. She loved to cook and care for her family. With somber faces we all gathered around the oval table in our cheery kitchen.

As I ate, memories flashed through my mind of happy times in this home—playing games, having songfests, and listening to the phonograph that Dad had won, along with one hundred records, at the Clay County Fair. I thought of our grove where we played hide-and-seek, of the pasture where we waded in the creek and of our pretty yard with its tire swing. How I would miss them! Most of all, I would miss our friends, relatives and our two grandmas who lived nearby. As I was a shy child, moving was intimidating.

Stars had winked out into dawn during breakfast. Sunlight was glistening on frosted trees and snowbanks when Dad said, "We'd better go out and make sure everything is ready."

He and my brothers bundled up and hastened outdoors, returning at intervals to get warm.

Before long, Aunt Katie, cheerful as usual, arrived bearing a hearty casserole for our dinner. Uncle Roy and our grandmas followed. Each grandma had loaned Dad a small sum to help. Uncle Roy soon joined the men outside.

Of course, I was not allowed out that morning, but watched intermittently from a window. So I'm relating what was told to me by my family.

At about eight o'clock, a hundred or more heavily clad farmers began arriving in their battered trucks and cars. Sober and concerned, some gathered in small groups to discuss the situation. Others inspected the sale items. Black glances followed the banker wherever he went. One irate farmer brought a hay rope and flung it over a tree limb—intending to hang the banker! Fortunately, others dissuaded him.

The auctioneer, bluff and hearty, began chanting the sale at nine o'clock sharp. Often when the animals and implements essential for farming were called, whispers would waft through the crowd, "Don't bid! Bob will need that!" Instantly, Uncle Roy or a neighbor would shout, "Fifty cents," or "A dollar!" thus securing many of the items.

By eleven o'clock the sale was over. Thanks to the unexpected kindness of Uncle Roy and the neighbors, and the generosity of our grandmas, Dad was able to buy back dear Pet and most of his other former possessions. He was grateful to them all.

Jubilant smiles lighted all of our faces as we sat down to enjoy Aunt Katie's casserole that noon. The sale had exceeded all of Dad's expectations.

"I wouldn't have believed it," Dad declared. What a contrast between the despair of that morning and the relief of the afternoon.

Despite being sold out, Dad, Mother and all of us would soon begin new lives on another farm he'd leased some thirty miles northwest of Dickens, near Milford. It would be a new beginning for our parents after twenty years of farming in the same comm.-unity. They would begin again, with hope and faith that this time their persistence and hard work would be amply rewarded.

As for me, moving could be good, I decided. I would have a new home, another yard, a grove and a barn to play in. And maybe, just maybe, I could go to school.

And I did!

Marie Taylor Wells taught school for 34 years, often writing personal stories for reluctant readers. Her interests include writing stories and verses for her children, grandchildren and for holidays, reading, woodworking, painting and church activities. She has lived in Marathon for fifty years.

565451 EG

UNITED STATES OF AMERICA
OFFICE OF PRICE ADMINISTRATION
WAR RATION BOOK TWO
IDENTIFICATION

....
(Name of person to whom book is issued)

....
(Street number or rural route)

OFFICE
OF
PRICE ADM.

....
(City or post office)   (State)   (Age)   (Sex)

ISSUED BY LOCAL BOARD NO. ....

(County)   (County)

....
(Street address of local board)   (City)

By ....
(Signature of issuing officer)

SIGNATURE ....
(To be signed by the person to whom this book is issued. If such person is unable to sign because of age or incapacity, another may sign in his behalf)

WARNING

1   This book is the property of the United States Government. It is unlawful to sell or give it to any other person or to use it or permit anyone else to use it, except to obtain rationed goods for the person to whom it was issued.

2   This book must be returned to the War Price and Rationing Board which issued it, if the person to whom it was issued is inducted into the armed services of the United States, or leaves the country for more than 30 days, or dies. The address of the Board appears above.

3   A person who finds a lost War Ration Book must return it to the War Price and Rationing Board which issued it.

4   PERSONS WHO VIOLATE RATIONING REGULATIONS ARE SUBJECT TO $10,000 FINE OR IMPRISONMENT, OR BOTH.

OPA Form No. R-121   16—30862-1

Ration Book provided by Betty Hembd Taylor

A TIME TO TRY MEN'S SOULS

Maxine Steele

The bank closings happened first, followed by other calamities. I was born in 1922, so I well remember that day in October 1929. My father had hauled a few hogs to town to be sold. When he came home he brought my brother, sister and me each a candy bar, a very unusual thing for him to do. He told us, "Enjoy it, as it'll probably be the last one you'll get for a while."

The gravity in the tone of his voice made a definite impression on me.

We who lived on a farm raising crops and livestock were a little better off than the families that lived in town. We had cows for milk, hens to lay eggs and a few beef cattle. My dad was a good herdsman and my mother was very frugal. We had room to grow a garden, to can vegetables for winter use. We would butcher one or two hogs and possibly a yearling calf for meat. Our folks had to be careful with these resources. Our farm food could be bartered for groceries. Cream and eggs were often taken to town on Saturday night to exchange for staples.

Even though we had deposited money in the bank, it was not available for release. But occasionally one of the banks would give out ten percent or more of deposits to be used to buy kerosene for the lamps and lanterns. At night our family gathered around the kitchen table to read or do school work by lamplight. A coal-wood-cob-burning stove stood in the middle of the room. It was a cookstove, but also the only source of heat for the house in winter. Isinglass panels in the door allowed us to watch the flickering flames inside.

Coal for such stoves was shipped by rail cars. Instead of buying coal, we sometimes saved money by having the whole family walk up and down the tracks to pick up any pieces of coal that had dropped off the cars.

No one used the parlor very often, so it was a useless expense to try to heat it. Our bedroom was above the parlor, and it was cold in our room. At night in the winter the bedroom windows were thick with frost. When we got up, we'd grab our clothes and hurry to the kitchen to dress where it was warm.

My folks raised ducks and geese, which ate grass most of the year and were fed cracked corn to fatten them up as food for the family.

Each winter our folks would fill one barrel with twenty dressed geese. The process sounds primitive these days, but only the feathers were removed, and the geese were shipped by rail car whole, with entrails included and the heads still attached. There were a lot of rich people from Europe in Chicago. Buying a goose meant one was of the upper class. Good thing somebody wanted them, as it gave us a bit of money for use during the winter.

We also dressed chickens and ducks for ourselves. Not even a feather got away from my mother if it could possibly be used elsewhere. Chicken feathers stuffed our pillows and freshly threshed straw was used to stuff our mattresses.

One of the things I remember was playing with a U-shaped magnet, probably four inches in height. It was a telephone magnet used in the old crank wall phones. A telephone line typically had eight to ten families on one line.

Since the women rarely got off the farm, they used the phone for entertainment, and tried to hear all the conversations. The more people listening in on the line, the weaker the signal grew. Occasionally the telephone operator would have to break in and ask the people to hang up as the signal was too weak for anyone to hear.

Each family had a code so the operator would know who was calling. Ours was 2-5-2 F20, which meant two short rings, 5 meant a longer ring, and then two more short rings. The F20 was the code number for our line. Sounds complicated today, but we kids thought it was pretty nifty to have our own code ring. At times of emergencies the operator would put out a general ring.

Mother loved to milk cows. It was one way for her to get outside. My sister helped with the milking while it was my job to feed and water the chickens, ducks and geese.

The kitchen table was covered with oilcloth so Mother never left the lamp on the table while she was outside. Instead we had a bracket lamp. A bracket was mounted high on the wall, with a concave mirror behind the lamp. This caused a magnified beam that could be turned wherever we wanted the light to shine.

The dust storms from 1934 through 1936 were devastating. They were called "black blizzards," with winds of 60 miles per hour and more. The winds swept across the crop ground, which had been already stripped by grasshoppers, picking up any small branches or tumbleweeds along the way. The dust would become so thick inside the house that we needed to light a lamp even during the day. Many would wet handkerchiefs and tie them across their faces so they could breathe without dust getting into their lungs.

During the summer months temperatures rose and we were hot and uncomfortable. One night my sister and I pulled our bed over to the windows to catch any stray breeze to cool us off. When we awoke in the morning we were covered with black dust.

My parents couldn't always get to church, but one Sunday my dad had my brother take my sister and me to Sunday school in the buggy. We were about two miles out of town, headed for home, when we saw a black cloud of dust in the southwest, advancing toward us.

The horses picked up the pace. They didn't like the dust in their eyes and lungs any more than we did. Being a good team, they knew where to go and headed straight for the barn. Luckily we reached home before the worst of the storm hit us.

The Depression years were followed by World War II. During the war years we had ration stamps to purchase sugar and meat. We sold some of our lard and also saved bacon drippings and unused lard, which was somehow used to manufacture explosives.

By 1947 the Rural Electification Corporation was able to get enough wire to start wiring farm places. Depression and war times were over, and rationing lessened, so tires and food could be obtained.

Truly these were the times to try men's souls. We who lived through the Depression and war years all agree we would not want to repeat those times. But we were all in the same boat, so to speak, and by working together and helping each other we coped during those stress-filled years.

Maxine Steele was born on a farm near Hartley, Iowa. She and her husband, Bob, have six children, ten grandchildren, and four great-grandchildren. Her life has been shaped in part by having had polio as a toddler, and dealing with post-polio issues. She spent a great deal of time and effort researching and writing about the dreaded disease, once known as infantile paralysis. Much of her research has been archived at the State Library of Iowa and the Iowa Historical Society. She has written for the Sioux City Journal and the Hartley Sentinel. Maxine and Bob are current residents of the Community Memorial Care Center in Hartley, Iowa.

THE GOOD OL' DAYS

Marlene Schoelerman

I'm from Havelock, a little town in northwest Iowa with a population of about two hundred and fifty. When I lived there as a girl we had a store, post office, hardware store, tavern, locker plant, barber shop, library, gas station, car repair shop, bank, theater, drugstore, a Methodist church, and even a blacksmith shop. So although we were a small community, we really had everything we needed.

My very good friend, Joan, and I had the job of cleaning the theater every week. It wasn't hard work, and since we were only twelve years old at the time it was perfect for us. The job gave us a little spending money, and the fun part was when we were done. There was a stage with a piano on the side, where we would pretend we were movie stars as we danced and sang and even played a little bit on the piano. When we were through with our "acting jobs" we would go next door to the tavern to find Doc, the man who'd hired us, and collect our payment. Doc was usually there, having a glass of beer. We would stand beside him until he paid us our quarters, and out the door we would dash, giggling all the way.

Doc also mowed the cemetery, and he hired us to clip the grass around the tombstones with hand clippers. This wasn't as much fun as the theater job, but it paid us another quarter. It usually took a couple of hours to finish the clipping, and then came the good part. He'd let us drive his old four-door automobile around the cemetery until he was done with the mowing. I don't think we ever told our parents he let us drive around. If we had, I'm sure it would have been the end of that job for us.

Doc's car had a floor shift. Once in a while if the other person wasn't watching, Jane or I would shift the gear. This happened one day when we were nearly ready to go home. I shifted the gear in reverse. Joan started the car, didn't check the gear and we roared backwards. We felt a thump. Joan stopped the car and we looked at each other, then jumped out of the car to find Doc lying on the ground behind it. We had knocked him down.

Doc just looked up at us and said in his German accent, *"Mein Gott,* you couldda kilt me!"

Thank God we hadn't. Doc wasn't a small man. Joan and I joked that he was built like Santa Claus, and maybe that extra padding had protected him. As he struggled to his feet we were relieved to see that he wasn't seriously injured.

After our hard work, we'd go to the drug store and have a cherry Coke and maybe splurge and have a bag of Planters peanuts to go with the Coke.

Where else but small town Iowa could two girls spend their summers having so much fun?

Marlene Schoelerman loves small-town living, considering all the people who live there her friends.

RED COMFORT ZONE

Pat Phipps

For each of you I hope there's a place where you have felt completely safe and wonderful. For me that place was the huge red barn on my grandparents' farm. In every season at any age I could make a trip out to that nearly-sacred spot and feel secure.

When I was a pigtailed preschooler I climbed with great effort up the smooth-runged ladder that was nailed against the barn wall. In the hayloft there was always a friendly cat that would come to visit me. Often I was lucky on these barn visits and was delighted by a new batch of kitties to love. The tiniest littermates would stumble around, trying to get their footing in this new world. The soft hay made their landings safe. As they grew older I would wiggle my toes to entertain them. They would crouch, wiggling their furry bottoms, and make ferocious bounces, wrapping their fuzzy legs around my bare feet in mock feline power. The hours spent with those adorable babies were totally without care.

When I climbed back down the ladder, it was usually into the waiting arms of my uncle, who would gently chide me for climbing up to the loft alone. Uncle Bob was my first crush. He wore cowboy shirts, jeans, and boots. His broad shoulders felt reassuring as he lifted me down and gave me a quick hug.

The family dog, Chop-Chop, was always waiting for me and wagging happily in the alleyway. This was a pup my dad had brought home in his B-29 after the Berlin airlift. Nearly all of the men had brought home puppies, but our pup was the most unusual of the lot. He had a huge, sausage-shaped body and the short legs of a dachshund. His head was wide and snouted. He grew to be oversized except for the stubby legs which somehow remained typically dachshund. The poor dog looked almost embarrassed when he tried to run, because his stomach barely cleared the ground. While the other dogs from that flight grew to be beautiful boxers, German shepherds and greyhounds, Chop-

Chop was my own, and that made him beautiful in my eyes. He was just my loving, faithful pal. He stayed at the farm because we couldn't have him in town. I think he loved the barn as much as I did.

The various stanchions in the barn were supported by six-by-six timbers at eight-foot intervals on either side along the alleyway. This sturdy enclosure had been built to stand for a very long time. The wood was rubbed butter-smooth and brown on all of the edges where for decades cattle or horses had rubbed their huge necks.

The front pens on either side of the barn were also large. On one side was an area which often held young calves. On the opposite side was the enclosure where the bull was sometimes held.

"Don't go near the bull pen," they had warned.

But of course I had to climb up the side boards of his stall just once to see what had them all so determined to warn me. I was like that. I usually had to learn things the hard way.

I pushed, pulled and dragged a bale of hay closer to see the monster I could hear on the other side. I climbed up the bale on stubby little-kid legs. From a hesitant squat I slowly stood up on tiptoe on the bale, and looked right into the face of a huge, black demon. The ring in his nose stood straight out toward me as he huffed at me with gleaming terrible black eyes. He didn't move for a moment. . . and I couldn't.

Then the demon slowly lowered his head down and, pawing the ground and snorting rudely, bashed against the boards where I stood.

I had no idea what a bull was for or why on earth they wanted that horrible creature. I flew backward off the bale and ran to ask Uncle Bob another of my hundreds of 'why' questions. Uncle Bob said that old Boris served his purpose there on the farm, but he wouldn't say more. I asked my mother, grandmother and aunt, "Why in the world would they want a mean old thing like Boris around the place?" The answers I got were no more than mumbles, smiles, and a change of subject.

Next to the stall where Boris snorted and pawed there were several horse stalls. The first horse I learned to ride was old Babe. Uncle Bob would put on the saddle and bridle and lead me around the corral that was attached to the barn. I thought I was pretty special. It was the equivalent of a teenager learning to drive a car, I suppose.

Eventually I was given the reins, with quiet advice from my uncle as I walked Babe around in a circle.

Finally, I was ready for freedom. Uncle Bob saddled up Rex, the friskier steed, and we went for our first ride, leaving the safety of the yard. We rode together. My favorite cowboy and I rode out across the pasture as far as we could go. I felt so adult, almost like a queen on that swaybacked horse. What I didn't know at the time was that Babe was so old she probably would have had a heart attack if we'd tried to gallop. We didn't. It was a peaceful, safe ride on a perfect summer afternoon for a little girl with big ideas.

The next area behind the calf pen was a small room which was always kept quite clean. A huge metal milk separator stood like an armored sentry in the center of the room. The milk room and the grain-holding room next to it had full wooden doors with wooden sliding latches. All of the other areas had just half-doors. Those full doors seemed to give the rooms the added importance they deserved. In goes the grain...out comes the milk.

The grain room was filled with a loose mixture of oats and cracked corn. I loved the idea of helping with chores. Uncle Bob showed me how to use the huge wooden scoop to get the mixture to pour in front of the stanchions that lined the width of the barn. I would hurry to get the scoops and pour them in place as Uncle Bob opened the door and called to the cows waiting in the cattle yard. As the animals lumbered in, stuck their heads into the appropriate stanchions and began to eat, the upright bars around their necks were closed to hold them in place.

Now the real fun began. Uncle Bob took his three-legged stool from the wall and sat on it beside the first warm cow. He put his thick fingers around the fat teats and pulled in rhythm.

The milk squirted down into the waiting tin pail, making a kind of music. Very quickly cats of every size and color began to appear. Uncle Bob would take the teat, pull, aim, and shoot the spraying milk toward a waiting cat. He aimed the milk gradually higher and higher. The cats stood on their hind legs, forming a kind of chorus line with furry white mustaches. Soon the older kittens joined in, meowing for their turn at the treat. They jumped, turned, and sang out for more.

After a while Uncle Bob stopped spraying toward the cats. He began to draw more and more milk in an ever increasing cadence into the waiting bucket. The squirting sound grew slower and less intense until the cow had given her all.

Some milk was then poured into the trough for a feline dinner treat. Chop-Chop tried to have a sip, but the galley of cats hissed him away every time. He would have to wait.

Each cow was milked until the entire row was finished. By this time the barn seemed very warm and smelly to a little city girl. The cattle were let out, and slipped and clicked their way back out the door.

We then took the rest of the milk to the separator. We poured it in to begin the amazing process of removing the cream. One can with a tight tin lid was saved to go to the house for supper. The rest of the milk was put into metal cans which were nearly as big as the little girl watching. The cream was put into another tightly sealed can to go to the house. If all conditions were right and time allowed, we might make ice cream.

The next chore to do before we could go in for supper was much less pleasant, but it had to be done. I picked up the specially-shaped shovel and began the "poop duty," as my cowboy called it. If all of the cows would have hit the gutter in the cement the job would have been easier, but the huge critters had very poor aim and did their thing both coming and going, so the mess had to be scooped from the floor all the way to the doors. A cat or a dog can be trained, but not a cow. I sometimes considered trying it.

Eventually my times on the farm became less frequent. I went away to college, got married, and had our children. I still returned to the farm with my family when I could.

I remember sitting in the haymow, holding a patient old cat and sobbing when my husband was in Viet Nam. Somehow that "sit and cry visit" made me feel better and less lonely.

Another time I went to the barn to pray when we had a seriously ill baby. The comfort I always felt there remained. Just knowing that special place was there would be enough even when I couldn't visit in person. I would sigh, take a deep breath, and transport myself there mentally from wherever I happened to be.

As a grown woman I understood the purpose for Boris. I still enjoyed playing with the kittens, but liked even more watching as my children giggled and wiggled their toes for the kitten pounces. Our visits to the farm always included a trip to the barn. I would feel the smooth wood, enjoy the familiar smells and remember the many times I'd found solace there.

Eventually my grandparents were gone and my aunt and uncle owned the farm. Chop-Chop went to doggy heaven, where I'm sure he is beautiful. There were no cows to be milked. The separator I had turned and washed was in the yard, the tank filled with flowers. Babe went to some green pasture in the sky. Rex, once a strong, prancing horse, became as slow as Babe had been.

One day, quite unexpectedly, came one of the hardest losses I have faced. My husband and I were taking our growing family back to the farm for a visit. As we went down the last road the children were chattering about the possibility of a new batch of kittens in the barn and the new puppy we would meet. Old Rex still let the little ones have a slow walk around the cattle yard with my aging cowboy uncle leading him.

We turned in to the familiar lane and looked ahead. For a long moment I didn't understand.

There was an empty space where the barn had been. All we saw was a field of corn stretching all the way to the skyline. The big red barn was gone.

I said hello to my aunt as she came out onto the porch to greet us. I left the children there, chattering with her as she showed them the new dog.

I walked alone to where that wonderful barn had been. My safest place was gone. The cement, smooth boards, a haven for animals, milk and feed, the fences—all were gone. Nothing but the growing corn field was there.

I felt my husband's presence as he came up behind me. He put his arms around me and we looked out across the field where the barn had been. I knew he understood what I was feeling. I cried like that little girl of long ago.

Life keeps changing. My huge red comfort zone was forever gone.

Pat Phipps spent her career as a teacher and was lucky enough to teach every grade and every age from three to seventy-three years. She and her husband, Jerry, have five children and twelve grandchildren. She wrote for area newspapers as a columnist and feature writer for more than twenty years. A few years ago she published her first book, *My Grandma Always Told Me*, and another book is in the works.

Drawing by LaVonne M. Hansen

INCOMING

Loren Gaylord Flaugh

The first eighteen years of my chance-filled life were spent on a 160-acre farm south of Archer, a small community in northwest Iowa's O'Brien County. The primary sustenance from our family farm in the middle 1950s came from selling the grain that Mother Nature and the nutrient-rich black soil provided. What livestock we raised was usually for 4-H projects or our own consumption.

My parents, Bernard and Lillian Flaugh, had a brood of four children, with another coming along much later in life.

One area of our farmstead afforded me, my brother and our two sisters endless hours of pleasure. A rather large, dense grove of trees blocked winter's bitterly cold, snow-laden winds. What a delightful playground lay out from the back door.

Our grove also afforded our family security, or so we kids imagined. Back in the Cold War's early days, whether or not the Russians were coming was always of grave concern. From the bunkers, forts, and tunnels we children had built in our grove, we felt our defensive fortifications would surely ward off any Russian army's intent of seizing our land. France's Maginot Line was no less formidable than ours.

But as the years passed, the grove began to shrink, tree by tree. Economics had forced my parents' hand, and more black soil was needed to be plowed under so a few more acres could become tillable. My siblings and I didn't like seeing our playground plowed under, but we had no say in the matter. Wildlife—the deer and the pheasants—didn't like it either.

Ours was a farmstead in transition. As the grove became smaller, a modern, single-story brick home was built to replace the wooden, two-story structure. Grandpa Stangeland was the house's head design engineer and general construction foreman. Grandpa didn't believe in using rebar in the cement—railroad *rails,* mind you, worked much better. Grandpa came from the old country, Norway, and he built a very sturdy, warm house.

Watching the menfolk in the family clear away an area of trees proved entertaining in its own enthralling way. Trees were felled and pushed into a huge pile by mighty and powerful bulldozers. Because I was infatuated with large machinery at an early age, to me, any bulldozer was mighty. The giant piles of wood were then set fire 'til only ashes remained. Rooting out the tree stumps and root balls was the hazardous part of the yearly project and the last thing done before the area was plowed under for row crops.

The last inconvenient trees that were removed were those immediately behind the machine shed and the round grain storage bin. While these few trees were still seventy-five yards from the new house, that distance would not be enough to keep us kids safe and out of harm's way. Fifteen feet was all that would prevent four little kids from being unlucky subjects of a most unlikely tragedy.

Dynamite was used to dislodge the firmly-held stumps. A wild guess apparently was how they determined the size of the explosive charge to use. Sometimes the calculations were grossly miscalculated.

We kids were sent to the ditch south of the house to watch the noisy activity from a safe distance. We were a good 100 yards from all the action, and what a grand time we were having, watching the geysers of dirt, roots, and wood being thrown high into the sky. With each explosion tree stumps flew every which way. One unguided missile even crashed into the steel grain bin, leaving it with a king-sized dent.

Since it was felt we were still in harm's way, my siblings and I were summarily ordered to retreat to the presumed safety of the house. We ran to the house and dashed for the northwest bedroom. Our new vantage point brought us fifty yards closer to ground zero.

With our little noses glued to the bedroom's two windows, we watched the men prepare to blow another stump. After the fuse was lit the men hurriedly retreated to what was deemed to be a safe distance.

The explosive force from the blast launched the tree stump into a suborbital trajectory, with God determining the landing site. Contrary to popular historic thinking and belief about who won the race to launch the first artificial moon, we did beat Sputnik! Almost.

The explosion lifted several hundred pounds of wood and dirt high into the sky, so high that it went completely out of sight. Inside the house, we didn't know that the soaring stump's trajectory had sent it over our heads. Simply put, the stump's re-entry was directly above the house and it was falling rapidly.

A split second later, the plummeting stump crashed through the roof of our new house. Wood and sheetrock tore and splintered. A tremendous thud reverberated throughout the house. The noise was awful. The stump plowed through the living room ceiling and bounced up off the cement floor before pummeling the couch and punching a hole through a living room wall, all in less time than it takes to blink twice. The house shook. An earthquake? In Iowa? No way!

We raced out from the bedroom. To our total wonderment, the living room couch was rolled over and the stump lay on the far side. It had scored a direct hit on our new home's living room floor, a mere fifteen feet from where we had been. The room looked like a federal disaster area.

The ceiling and roof were opened up to the heavens. The chandelier in the room's center had been wiped out. It never stood a chance. But Grandpa's thick cement floor stopped the stump's momentum cold.

The men raced for the house when they saw where the errant stump had impacted. They feared someone had been hurt, or even worse, killed. But chance played a critical role in that no one was seriously injured.

When all the excitement abated, the several-hundred-pound stump was cut up and carted back outside. The men climbed up on the roof and covered the hole with a green tarp.

For many days and weeks after, our house was the focus of many head-scratching curiosity seekers. Strangers and ordinary gawkers wandered by and some even came inside to get a closer look.

Not until four decades later would I learn that Harold Stofferan, Sanborn's dirt contractor, was the man in charge of calculating how much dynamite to use that day. During a conversation with Bill Stofferan some years ago, Bill told me that he still recalls watching his father write the check for the repairs to our home.

Loren Gaylord Flaugh is someone always drawn to real-life stories where extreme coincidence or destiny is the central element of the story.

THE STORM OF THE CENTURY

Kermit H. Dietrich

November 11, 1940, is known to Minnesota historians as the date of the "Storm of the Century." That day started as a very warm, Indian summer day. People went about their daily lives wearing lightweight clothing, as there were no warning signs for the approaching storm. Duck hunters traveled early from the cities to their favorite lakes or swamps to await sunrise and the opening of the hunting season. Most of them had not yet winterized their cars by putting alcohol in their fuel for cold weather starts.

The stage was set for tragedy. Snow started late in the morning, heavy and wet. By about noon, when the temperature started dropping and the wind came at gale force, people realized that this was a serious storm. Many hunters froze in their boats and duck blinds or perished in cars that wouldn't start.

When the storm hit I was in my one-room country schoolhouse, the Beacon Light School, District 77. I was in the fifth grade, and I was ten years old. Our teacher, Miss Bergstrom, taught all of the grades, first through eighth. Seeing the storm coming, she wisely sent my classmates home around noon.

I stayed because Miss Bergstrom and I lived on the same road, about a mile from the school. She tried to walk me home. Deep drifts had already piled up on the road. At first we walked in the adjacent woods, as this area was somewhat sheltered from the strong winds. As we struggled through the snow, Miss Bergstrom held tightly to my mittened hand. After about a quarter of a mile of trudging through the blinding and ever-deepening snow, she exclaimed, "We'll never make it!"

We turned around, barely making it back to the Beacon Light School.

Once inside we warmed up a bit with the remaining heat from the woodstove, then we set out again, walking to a farmhouse about two blocks west of the school. There we were welcomed by the Piepers, an elderly couple who were always prepared for the worst kinds of weather. They had plenty of their own hand-hewn firewood and lantern oil, and their basement was stacked with a bounty of sturdy Mason jars filled with vegetables from Mrs. Pieper's garden.

After a comforting supper of meat, potatoes, gravy, and canned peas, Miss Bergstrom and I sat and talked with the Piepers about our brush with death in the storm that was still raging outside. At this point in the storm the roads were impassable. It got dark early, and after a while Mrs. Pieper announced, "It's time for bed."

Though I should have just been thankful for my life and for a safe and warm place to sleep, I was suddenly gripped with a terror such as I had never experienced. Was I going to have to sleep with Miss Bergstrom? I was certain that the small farmhouse had only one room upstairs, and as they'd had only one child, they most certainly had just one bed in that solitary bedroom.

Mrs. Pieper headed up the dark stairs with a kerosene lamp in one hand, leading me along with the other. Miss Bergstrom was behind me, cutting off my means of escape.

Climbing the stairs seemed to take forever. My mind was filled with dread at the thought of my older brother and my classmates later discovering that I had slept with Miss Bergstrom!

I would sooner have been remembered as the kid who'd perished in the snowstorm.

At the top of the stairway was a small landing. I saw the closed door, leading to the dreaded bedroom. My heart quaked.

Mrs. Pieper turned to me and pointed to a steep-roofed corner off of the landing and said, "Kermit, you can sleep there." In that lamp-lit corner was a spare twin bed with a small lumpy mattress filled with dried cornhusks.

Never since have I experienced such relief or comfort at such a simple blessing. My worst fears had been averted. I slept soundly that night on the cornhusk bed which crackled beneath me whenever I moved.

My parents didn't find out until the following day, when I was finally able to walk home, that I'd survived the storm. They had prayed for my safe return and were very relieved to see me. I probably owe my life to Miss Bergstrom's quick decision to turn back in that storm. But I'll always remember November 11, 1940, as a time of terror when I almost had to sleep with the nice teacher we secretly referred to as "Old Lady Bergstrom."

She was in her late twenties at the time.

Kermit H. Dietrich is a 79-year-old retired dairy farmer living in Waconia, Minnesota. He was persuaded by his daughter, Christine Lindemer, to write down some of the stories he told her while she was growing up and submit them for publication.

Photograph by Dan Ruf

CALM BEFORE THE STORM

Diane Schulze

It was another steamy humid day in central Iowa with no relief in sight. Box fans roared in the open windows to circulate hot, sticky air around the living room. As I sat quietly, trying not to generate any extra heat, sweat rolled down the nape of my neck. I swept a wet washcloth over it. I lived in an older house with its rock foundation, built in the early 1900s by my great-grandparents. It contained no air conditioning.

But I loved the old house, with its creaky sloping floors, my small, confined bedroom and memories of my ancestors who'd lived here before me. My great-grandpa had been six feet tall, long and lanky, with skin weathered from farming forty acres with his muscular draft horses, Pete and Buck. Great-grandma had tended her chickens and garden, and had made hearty home-cooked meals for her five children. Their pioneer spirit still fills every corner of the old house.

The weather alert warning on TV pierced the air. "The National Weather Service has issued a tornado watch for the following counties in central Iowa: Dallas, Greene, Boone, Story and Polk. The chance for tornados, damaging winds and hail exists. Please stay tuned for further bulletins."

A collective groan in the room set the tone for the approaching storm.

"I hope we aren't going to be up again all night, unable to sleep, with all the thunder and lightening," my mother said. She was petrified of storms and grew nervous whenever a weather alert was announced.

Striding to the window, my dad studied the sky. He grabbed his cap, slapped it on his head and hastened out the back door. After a few minutes the door swung open again and I heard his commanding voice. "Diane, come outside. I want to show you some things."

I followed him out the door, to the center of the back yard. Peering upward, I was shaken by the sight of rolling, ominous black clouds building in the west. Jagged bolts of lightning were shooting toward the ground, followed by the crack of thunder. Tints of deep green brushed the clouds, pink and violet setting the pallet of the sky. The stillness of the air was stifling, as though the oxygen had been sucked out of it. Birds had ceased to sing and not a leaf or a blade of grass twitched. After a few minutes of this the wind came up, and changes began to take place around us.

"I want you to learn the signs of the weather," Dad said. "Can you feel what the wind is doing? It's shifting direction."

Cold air from the north raised goose bumps on my arms, sending a chill into my spine, while from the south the steaminess stung my skin.

"Now take a deep breath and tell me what smell you detect," Dad told me.

I inhaled. A slight sulfuric odor, as though a match had been blown out, lingered in the air.

"What does this all mean?" I asked. Panic was beginning to set in, as I'd learned from my mom to fear storms. "Why do I need to know this?"

Dad said, "You need to know how to read the weather and be aware of what's going to occur before it drops on top of you. If you wait for the radio or TV to tell you, it could be too late. Look at the sky over Ankeny."

I looked. My eyes grew to the size of saucers. A pointed cylindrical cloud was dipping down, retracting, and dipping again. Wait, over there, another one! My mind was reeling, my heart pounding. I could no longer catch my breath. The wind increased as it sheared through the leaves on the trees, their branches creaking and groaning.

"Go get your mom. Now!" he commanded. "We have to go to the cave."

Mom was already halfway out the door, with transistor radio and candles in hand. We descended the rough concrete steps into the musty darkness of the storm cellar. I heard the sizzle of the candle lighting as my dad closed and latched the door above us. We huddled close on our folding stools and I cringed at the sight of a salamander waddling toward a rough wooden shelf, then disappearing beneath it. Mom turned on the radio. At first we heard the broadcast, but it quickly changed to only static.

"Go ahead and turn off the radio and listen quietly," Dad said in a matter-of-fact voice.

The wind was howling above us and the rumble in the distance was unnerving. The railroad tracks were just a mile from our house. I waited for the whistle of a freight train, but it didn't come. The rumbling continued and the wind intensified. There was a deafening thud on the cave door and the sound of shattering glass. This was immediately followed by the thundering sound of hail. I covered my ears against the crashing above us.

"Is it ever going to stop?" I cried. It had been only minutes but felt like hours.

Then the winds died down, the hail and rain ceased and the rumble in the distance was gone. All was suddenly still again.

Dad made his way up the steps. He unlatched the heavy, damp door, heaving it upward with his shoulders. Broken glass slid across the door's surface. The fading rays of the evening sun peeked through the remaining clouds.

We surfaced, stepping through the doorway, glass crunching beneath our shoes. Our fifty-five gallon metal barrel, which was used to store canning jars, had created the thud on the cave door. It had settled snugly against the north side of the house, eight feet from the cave.

Hail the size of golf balls covered the ground. Each hailstone had half-inch prongs over its surface. Gathering a few to put in the freezer as proof, my dad explained that the hail was a sign that one or both of the funnel clouds we'd seen had touched down.

"Your great-grandparents would have known these signs," he said. "They had no warning systems like we have now. This old house has stood through many storms over the years, and it always comes out unscathed. They don't build houses like this anymore, that'll stand up to everything nature throws at them."

"That's because they're still here in spirit, protecting us, Dad," I said.

He laughed, and continued to gather his hail. Mom had already gone back into the house.

Exhausted by the wrath of the storm we'd just experienced, we retired to our beds early that night. My sleep was fitful. I tossed and turned, reliving the events of the day, over and over. Once, hearing a rumble in the distance, my body stiffened and I held my breath, straining to hear. Ah, there was the mournful whistle of the train. Exhaling deeply, I fell into a deeper sleep.

First thing the next morning, I had Driver's Education. I met the other student drivers—my classmates Susan, Cheryl and Laura—at the school, where we waited until our instructor pulled up in the well-marked Driver's Education car.

"Ladies, we're going to drive through Ankeny today," he said in an arrogant tone we knew well. "I want to see the damage the tornado caused last night."

"I don't think we can get in," I protested. "The roads are blocked off going into Ankeny. The news said only authorized personnel would be permitted through. It could be dangerous with all the debris."

He was agitated by our resistance. "I'm a Driver's Ed instructor and that's all the authorization I need," he said. "Now, get in the car. Laura, you'll drive first today."

Laura got behind the wheel and drove the car from the gravel parking lot. We rode in silence, each questioning in our minds the images we might possibly see. The closer we got to the city limits the more debris we encountered. Laura slowed down. We were in a line of cars, all trying to enter town. Some of the cars ahead of us turned around and passed us going the other direction. When it was our turn, Laura slowly pulled up next to the police car parked at the barricades. He motioned us through, and our instructor chuckled at his victory.

"Turn onto Ankeny Boulevard to the left," he said. "Stay in the center lane. I'll tell you where to turn next."

I was having visions of news clips I'd seen about Viet Nam. We'd entered a war zone. Broken branches, shattered glass and splintered boards littered the streets and walkways. Toppled light poles, snapped electrical lines and makeshift rolling stop signs lined the intersections. Buildings were missing sections of their roofs, and windows had been blown out. The electricity was out.

"Turn left at the next corner, Laura, and be careful of the dump trucks and end-loaders," our instructor said.

Laura obeyed his commands. She continued to weave back and forth through the obstacles in the road. As we approached the residential area most heavily hit, we gasped. An entire house was gone. Nothing was left except the block foundation. The houses on either side remained standing, but with missing shingles, broken windows and signs of structural damage. On the opposite side of the street, diagonally in line with the first missing house, was another vacant lot, only a foundation left as evidence a house had once been there.

How could this be? A tear ran down my cheek. I quickly brushed it away, hearing my dad's words of the night before: "They don't build houses like this anymore."

I wondered what these people would do, where they would stay. How could one storm cause so much massive destruction?

The F4 tornado of June 18, 1974, that crashed through Ankeny left a lasting impression on my mind. It was neither the first tornado nor the last to devastate the Heartland of America, but it will remain in our memories.

My experience was a well-taught lesson in survival. The old house remains standing after all these years, worn and beaten by time, but unscathed by the storms it has endured. I still hear the whisper of my father's voice: "They don't build houses like this anymore."

Diane Schulze grew up in central Iowa and lives with her husband, Ted, in rural Jasper County. She continues writing her memories and the stories passed down to her for future generations.

UPHILL BOTH WAYS

Ted Paulsen

My Grandpa William went to Colony School. It was a one-room schoolhouse located out in the country in Benton County, Iowa. There was no electricity and no running water. Grandpa's school had an outhouse that was one hundred and fifty feet from the schoolhouse.

School started at 7:30 a.m. and ended at 3:00 p.m. Before Grandpa went to school each day he had to milk the dairy cows and separate the milk from the cream. After he finished his chores he had to walk a mile and a half through the fields and over two barbed-wire fences to get to school. School was rarely called off. If the teacher could make it, they still had school. That meant my grandpa walked through snow, rain and all kinds of weather. According to Grandpa, the walk was uphill both ways.

The usual clothes that boys wore at Colony School were overalls and long-sleeved shirts. When the weather was warm most kids didn't wear shoes. Grandpa claims this made his feet tough enough to walk on cockleburs.

At school every kid had a job to do. If you'd been in trouble you might get the job of going to the basement to get the coal to heat the schoolhouse for that day. Another job was to fetch water from a neighbor's well. The best jobs were ringing the bell at the start of school or raising the flag. Only the kids who hadn't been in trouble got those jobs.

Grandpa William studied eight subjects. They were math, science, spelling, geography, reading, penmanship, history and English. Grandpa's favorite subject was mathematics because it was the easiest for him. His least favorite subject was English, which he thought was hardest. There was one teacher at his school. She taught everyone, from kindergarten through eighth grade. In fact, my grandpa had only two different teachers during the whole eight years he went to Colony School.

When he was in the seventh grade his teacher said, "William, unless you straighten out you'll never make 'er in high school."

Well, he did straighten out, because after the eighth grade at Colony School my grandpa went on to Atkins High School, where he graduated as Salutatorian.

Grandpa had two recesses each day that were thirty minutes long. During recess, he played tag, hopscotch, Red Rover, and Ring-around-the-Rosie. They didn't have a jungle gym or a slide. My grandpa's favorite thing to do during recess was to play in a deep ditch where the teacher couldn't see him. All the kids made their own fun.

On the walk home from school he got into more trouble than he did at school. There were creeks to play in and sisters to splash. One time he got into big trouble at school. When he was in the seventh grade he didn't have money to buy cigarettes, so he invented his own. He twisted up corn silks and wrapped them in a corn husk. He went to the outhouse at school and tried smoking his corn husk cigarette in there. When he lit it the fire burned faster than he thought it would. Before he knew it he had burned down the entire outhouse!

My grandpa is a pretty funny guy and to this day when a doctor asks about his smoking history, he tells the doctor, "I quit in the seventh grade."

Ted Paulsen is a 7th-grader in Iowa City, Iowa, where he lives with his family and his dog, Louie. Ted wrote "Uphill Both Ways" when he was in 5th grade.

UNCLEAN UNCLEAN

Troy Van Beek

Not many children walk to school anymore. It's sad, and may be due in part to the horror stories told about two-mile walks through knee-deep snow, uphill both ways.

Not all walks to school and home were like that however. Some could be downright fun.

My father grew up in Sioux County just a little west of Sioux Center, Iowa. His walk to school was not two miles and it was not uphill both ways. It was three-quarters of a mile on a fairly level grade. A group of boys, two sets of brothers, made the daily jaunt to country school in the morning and home again at the end of the day. The building was a typical one-room schoolhouse with clapboard siding. A sign hung above the front door that proclaimed in black block letters: West Branch #2.

There was just one room inside, used for teaching each class of five to seven students ranging from kindergarten through eighth grade. The student body consisted of around twenty-five students.

Each day my dad Virgil and his brother Irwin would meet up with another set of brothers, Dale and Ron, along the road to school. They were an athletic bunch of boys and in the spring baseball gloves were carried along to the school for recess time and ball-playing. According to the story, the ball-playing some-times took place in the long hallway in the school building, and this is where the story starts getting good.

At the end of the hallway was the boys' bathroom. Because West Branch #2 was a little more modern than most country schools it had indoor chemical toilets. The chemical toilets did, however, resemble an outhouse. There was no hole in the ground, but there was a tank in the basement beneath the privy. Those who attended country schools equipped with these facilities will no doubt know what I'm describing. It was a basement-dwelling tank of raw sewage into which chemicals were dumped to keep the odor in check.

On this particular day a game of hallway catch turned into a game of hallway horseplay among the four boys. My dad doesn't fully remember, but he thinks they began playing keep-away with one of the boys' new baseball glove. In the midst of the game the new glove sailed past the youthful ballplayer who stood in front of the open door of the boys' bathroom, and with a definite "plop" the glove found its way into the tank by way of a toilet seat that had been left up.

Now, I've played the game of keep-away before and I have been "it," but I've never lost a new baseball glove to the bowels of a chemical toilet. I imagine the owner of the glove was upset. At the moment of the "plop" all the fun that was being had turned immediately into Mission Impossible. "Gentlemen, your mission, should you choose to accept it, is the ultimate retrieval of the gunky glove that is floating in the septic tank."

The boys procured a stick, possibly a broomstick borrowed from the janitor's closet. With turned-up noses and stick in hand, they began poking into the unknown. They fished the glove from its abode in the commode. The glove came out covered in goo and made its way outside of the West Branch #2 to wait for the end of the day.

The owner of the glove did not have to play the outfield that afternoon. However, the glove had to get home. The boys did not relish carrying the gooey glove in their hands, so the stick went along and four boys headed home with their books under their arms and the glove on a stick.

While the walk may not have been two miles or uphill both ways, there was still some time to kill on the three-quarter mile journey home and a new game was invented. The bearer of the stick discovered that it made a wonderful instrument that could fling a filth-covered, leather-fingered projectile in such a way that a satisfying "splat" was heard when the glove hit the back of one of the other walkers. The game was made more fun by the fact that the dirty glove left a stinky stain on the clothing of the boy who was on the receiving end of the projectile.

Soon it was not enough to just throw the glove. A war cry had to be issued.

"Unclean, unclean," the flinger would yell before whipping the glove at a walker. Over the course of the three-quarter mile walk the glove became caked with the gravel of the road along with the original muck from the depths of West Branch #2 boys' toilet.

Walking home from school in the old days was not always drudgery. It could be fun. I imagine four boys laughing and running along a gravel road just a little west of Sioux Center. They drop their books so both hands can be employed to acquire the moving target and fling the glove.

They shout with glee, "Unclean, unclean," and then—SPLAT!

Troy Van Beek grew up in northwest Iowa where he developed a love for the outdoors and for listening to stories. His love of listening has turned into a love of telling. He's grateful to his wife Pam and daughter Courtney for giving their ear to this "want to be" storyteller.

Photo provided by Judy Taber

SPECIAL DISPENSATION

Roger Stoner

Turning fourteen years old in 1966 made it a very important year for me. Being fourteen meant I could get my learner's permit and take Driver's Education. A learner's permit and passing Driver's Ed were the two requirements for obtaining a real driver's license, which was the most important goal of every teenager living in my small northwest Iowa town.

The Driver's Education course consisted of three weeks in the classroom and then three weeks of actual driving with our instructor, Mr. Fullmer, who was also our high school superintendent. The classes were boring for most of us. Mr. Fullmer tried to make them interesting, but we just sat at our desks as he covered the basics over and over. Each of us believed we already knew how to drive.

"Use both hands to steer," Mr. Fullmer stated in his deep baritone as he demonstrated. "Place the left hand at ten o'clock and the right hand at two o'clock on the steering wheel. Slow the vehicle before turning, using the hand-over-hand method to turn the wheel."

He demonstrated a right turn with his imaginary steering wheel by rotating his left hand from ten o'clock to two o'clock and bringing his right hand over to grasp the wheel and rotate it down to three o'clock while bringing his left back again to twelve and rotating, then reaching up to twelve again with his right hand. He repeated the procedure until we were all nearly dizzy from turning this imaginary circle. He taught us the fundamentals of running the clutch and shifting a manual transmission and repeatedly went over the rules of the road, covering everything we would need to know to pass our drivers' tests. But we were all impatient to get behind the wheel. We had two years to learn all that crap. We wanted to drive!

When our first week to leave the classroom finally came and we actually got to drive the car, we were all excited, yet somewhat nervous. I was a little more nervous than the other kids, perhaps because I had a plaster cast on my left arm that ran from mid-palm to just short of my elbow. The cast was heavy and got in the way, especially when I was using the hand-over-hand method to turn. Each time I made a turn, the clumsy cast caused me to bump the steering wheel and then honk the horn.

My turns usually sounded something like, "Bump-*beep*, bump-*beep*, bump-*beep*," which caused the students riding in the back seat to break up with hilarity. They laughed a lot while I was driving. It got so bad that Mr. Fullmer decided to give me a "special dispensation" from using the hand-over-hand method and let me turn the wheel by just rotating it with my right hand.

And let me tell you, it was much cooler to spin that steering wheel with one hand than it was to hand-over-hand it. The other students thought I was lucky to get special dispensation. But they didn't know how lucky I really was.

Another reason 1966 was an important year was that I was finally old enough and big enough to hire out to area farmers to help shell corn. Back in those days most of the farmers still picked their corn with corn-pickers and stored the ears in corncribs. After spring planting was finished, it was common practice to hire a man with a corn-shelling machine and a couple of boys from town to rake and scoop the ears of corn from the crib into the sheller, which separated the kernels from the cobs. The corn was then trucked to the grain elevator for sale. It was good, steady work for the summer because the farmers had to empty the cribs to create storage space for their new corn crop.

Yes sir, it was going to be a good year. I was going to take Driver's Ed and make a lot of money shelling corn and baling hay. I'd probably start saving up to buy a car. . .

What is it they say about even the best-laid plans often going astray?

We had started shelling corn long before Driver's Ed started. The first job was notable because it was my friend Craig's first time working for a farmer. The corn-sheller operator, Walt, was quick to tell us that he was "not a nice man." He used the most colorful language we'd ever heard to instruct us in connecting the conveyor sections together and placing them in the corncrib next to the low, removable boards in the bin wall.

It took us slightly more than four hours to rake and scoop the corn from the crib into the conveyor. We stopped only for lunch or when the farmer had to replace the filled corn and cob wagons with empty wagons. The going rate for corn-shelling was one dollar per hour. When we were finished, the farmer made out a check for $4.50 and handed it to Craig, saying, "Put your John Hancock on this check and then I'll sign it."

Craig took the checkbook and began writing, but then a confused look came over his face. He asked, "How do you spell Hancock?"

On our next job the farmer's two young sons, with the help of their border collie, killed enough mice as they escaped from the corncrib to fill two paper grocery sacks. The highlight of the day came when the boys snuck up behind their mother as she was preparing to serve us dinner in her kitchen and shouted, "Hey, Mom, *look*!" as they shoved the bags full of bloody, dead mice up in her face.

We almost didn't get dinner.

The last corn-shelling job I had that summer came about a week before we were scheduled to start driving the car in Driver's Ed. It was one of those jobs where we were short-handed. The cob wagon was almost full and the farmer hadn't returned from dumping the other one. There was still some room in the corn wagon and we hated to shut down the sheller if the wagon wasn't yet full.

The corn-sheller operator told me to climb up and rake the cobs from one side of the wagon to make more room. I climbed up on the top and stumbled around in the shifting, rolling cobs as I raked them around, trying to utilize every bit of space. To make a long story short, when the wagon was full, I lost my footing and fell off.

During the first phase of the fall I used some of the colorful language I had learned from Walt that summer. But as I cleared the wagon, my mind noted that it was kind of like flying . . . down . . . with the eight long tines of the corn rake coming right at my face! At the last instant I threw the rake in my right hand away from me and reached out with my left hand to break my fall and, consequently, my left wrist.

So you see, that's why I had a cast on my wrist during Driver's Ed class and was lucky enough to still be around to receive a "special dispensation" from our instructor.

Very lucky, indeed.

Roger Stoner published *The Peterson Patriot* (Peterson, Iowa) for more than fifteen years, doing a lot of the writing, including his weekly column, "Roger's Remarks." He and his wife have two grown children and six wonderful grandchildren. He's been published in magazines, and is looking for an agent or publisher for his novel. He works for Eaton Corporation in Spencer, Iowa, and enjoys hunting, fishing, woodworking and wood carving.

SKUNKED

Harvey Chouanard

It was a cold autumn morning in central Minnesota when my mom got the call. A neighbor needed to rid her garage of an unwanted, probably sick, skunk. She knew that among the six Chouanard boys, all of whom loved to hunt, someone would be able to rid her garage of the pollutant. My brother and I had some time before school, and shooting medium-sized varmints was one of our favorite things to do. I believe it ranked somewhere between playing baseball and swimming. I'd just entered the ninth grade and chasing girls was a thought, but not yet an action. At that time it was more important to avoid the embarrassing punishment of "swirlies" or "wedgies" from upper classmen than to get a date. To avoid the humiliating punishments given by the high school echelon, a guy had to keep a low profile at all times.

After breakfast, my brother Wayne and I headed to the neighbor's garage. Wayne spotted the skunk huddled behind some boxes and promptly shot it. He slid the limp carcass on a shovel, being careful not to touch it for fear of transferring the skunk scent to himself. I walked behind Wayne, shuffling my feet and daydreaming, as usual. Wayne hiked ahead, dragging the shovel behind him. At some point he heaved the skunk into a ditch and we headed home to dispose of the shovel.

The autumn wind bit my cheeks as we began the two-block trek through downtown Nelson, Minnesota, to the bus stop. We crossed the railroad tracks near our house. Mom used to give sandwiches to the hobos that rode the rails. Sometimes, while we were playing tag in the stockyards, a scruffy, bearded man would lay money down on a piece of lumber. He'd tell us what he wanted and we'd run to the grocery store to fill the order. We'd then lay the food down on the rough lumber where it was promptly replaced by a nickel and sometimes a dime. Enough for an ice cream at the local bar that served ice cream, 3.2 beer, soda pop, and a greasy hamburger and fries—but only if you happened to enter when the cook happened to be working. The next day, the scruffy, bearded man might be replaced by a new scruffy, bearded man waiting his turn to ride the rails west for the winter.

Since Nelson didn't have a high school, the high school students caught the bus at the K-8 building. It was a two-story brick structure, surrounded by a field, and was considered fairly large compared to the other country schools in the area. My stint in the Nelson school brings back fond memories. I was the only boy, with twelve girls in my class. The girls loved to play predator and prey. Since I was always the only prey I became a very fast runner, which was useful during the Field Days our school hosted every year.

Field Day was held in the spring when the weather warmed up in the afternoon, but was still chilly in the early morning. Neighboring towns came by bus, van, or car and spent the day competing in an open, bumpy, and grassy field. I guess it would have been called Track and Field Day if we'd had a track. Still, we set up a high-jump between two rusty poles staked in the ground. We'd walk off the distance for the 50-, 100-, and 200-meter dashes and mark them with a flag attached to each stick. I won many of those races, thanks to the twelve young coaches who ambushed me daily.

The seven-mile bus ride to Alexandria High School was miserable when cold outside. The heat on the bus never seemed to work, which made arriving at school an actual pleasure.

When we got to school the morning after disposing of the skunk, I headed to my first-period class and sat at my desk. The pleasant hiss and click of the radiator warmed my chilled body as I waited for class to start. As my body thawed, I—and many people around me—began to notice a pungent odor.

"What is that smell?"

"Did a skunk die in here?"

A moment of panic set in at the faceless chatter that surrounded me. I realized the horrific odor everyone was talking about was coming from my skunk-scented shoes. The wonderful heat that thawed my body had also thawed the nasty scent on my shoes. I began to perspire and my heart beat faster. I certainly didn't want to carry the nickname "Skunk Boy" throughout my high school career. Walking around school smelling like skunk was not a good way to keep a low profile. I pictured myself being dunked in a toilet stained, if I was lucky, with rust.

I promptly asked to be excused. I left the room, while my classmates searched underneath their desks with wrinkled noses, trying to find the disagreeable smell. Downstairs in the boys' locker room I replaced my skunk shoes with my better-smelling sneakers. But my plan was not yet complete.

When the bell rang I dashed back down to the locker room, skipping sections of stairs in the process and mentally thanking my twelve "girlfriends" for preparing me for just this moment. I hurried past some confused football players who were inconspicuously smelling their own armpits, and shoved my skunk shoes into the paper bag I'd saved from my lunch.

On the bus ride home I nervously opened a window. The cold air felt good on my flushed face.

"Hey, it's too cold to open up windows!" said the bus driver. "Shut it!"

I nodded my head in accordance, but when his eyes glanced away from the rearview mirror back to the road, I launched the paper bag out the window. The wind whipped the bag and my shoes tumbled out into the ditch.

When I got home I told Mom the truth about my missing shoes. She was glad I'd disposed of them so she didn't have to. That smell would never have come out, she said, and she certainly didn't want skunk shoes in her house.

With one toss of a bag I'd managed to save my reputation while still keeping a low profile.

Harvey Chouanard grew up in the small town of Nelson, Minnesota. Now retired after forty-six years with the same company, he lives in Deephaven, Minnesota.

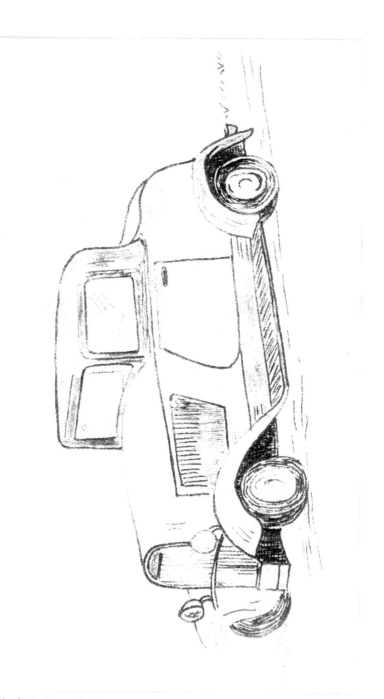

Drawing by LaVonne M. Hansen

EDUCATIONAL PIONEERING

Rev. Francis W. Mennenga

The year was 1948. High School was completed. So were the tests of seventeen subjects, according to state standards. I still needed twelve hours of education at Kearney State Teacher's College, Kearney, Nebraska. Then I would be eligible to teach in rural Nebraska schools. How I looked forward to beginning my professional life as an educator.

After earning the needed credits during the summer, I made my credentials known at the placement office at the college. A job opening in Kearney County, the county in which I lived, six miles south of Heartwell, Nebraska, sounded like the ideal location.

But in looking over the contract, I discovered a slight problem. The salary offer of $140 per month wasn't a problem. Nor was the prospect of paying $30 per month for room and board located just a quarter of a mile from the school grounds. No, the problem was that there was no school building. It had burned to the ground earlier in the summer. The problem was slight, I was assured, since a vacant building with the same floor plan would be moved to the location in time for the fall term.

I would have an enrollment of six students, a boy in kindergarten, a girl in third grade, a girl and a boy in fourth grade, and two male sixth graders. The school board authorized me to purchase the needed textbooks for classes at Baumgarten's Variety Store in Kearney, and things were beginning to fall into place. Relatives and friends, at my request, collected magazine covers, advertisements and anything else of artistic value to decorate the single room. I mounted the pictures on construction paper and displayed them all around the room. My students would be surrounded by colorful images to help make learning a pleasure.

After arriving at my new living quarters and receiving the key to the school building, I eagerly went to survey the situation.

Professor Nigh had warned our college reading class that our first word on the opening day of classes would probably be, "Well." She hadn't missed it by far. The building was intact, but it had been used for target practice before the move. The windows were notched with holes, and the ceiling held decorative tin squares often associated with church interiors in the area. Blackboards were attached to the front of the room, and Palmer handwriting placards were still above it, but there were no bookcases or shelves.

Though desks were attached to the floor and a potbelly stove stood in the middle of the room, this place needed more furniture. Orange crates and nail kegs were soon positioned as book holders and a place for a Red Wing water cooler. The front door opened to the coal and wood shed, and a concrete slab served as the entryway to the playground swings and the paths to the outhouses. It would do. It must.

Golda Canaday was the county superintendent for all the rural schools. She was instrumental in bringing a movie projector to the Heartwell Public School. The various schools in the area were invited, even urged, to attend. My used 1932 Plymouth coupe, which I called Carrie, seemed to be the only transportation available on those occasions. The students and I did what we could to avail ourselves of the educational advantages those showings offered us. How did we do it? Well, the two girls and the kindergartner rode up front with me, while the three boys would crawl into the trunk, which was propped open with a tree stump. Away we went, traveling the six or seven miles quite gleefully.

At Thanksgiving, art materials were provided for the students' artistic expression of gratitude. Before the art period was finished, the third-grade lass brought her project to me.

"I bet you can't guess what I'm thankful for, Mr. Mennenga," she said, holding up her project.

She was right, I couldn't guess. Her composition consisted of a mound of brown Crayola shading. It might have been dirt, the good earth. It might have been a mountain. But educational standards had suggested a teacher should not block any student's originality, but simply ask for an explanation. After complimenting the composition, I asked the girl her interpretation of the work of art. She was a stepdaughter of an area farmer who'd married a mother of two from Tennessee. Things were better for this little girl in Nebraska than they had been earlier in her life. Her response was not surprising, but never to be forgotten. She said, "Mr. Mennenga, I'm thankful for gravy over my potatoes."

In the fall, when it rained, it was necessary to cover the bullet holes in the windows. I accomplished this with blotters from the bank and tape to hold the wind and moisture out. The winter of 1949 was particularly harsh. We had several blizzards, and the wind whipped the snow above the tin squares serving as our ceiling. After I'd built a fire and the room began to warm, we needed buckets or gallon cans for the *drip, drip* here and the *drop, drop* there.

The year became routine, with the teacher carrying water for the cooler from the landlady's home, being custodian, building the fires and having the building warm as the children arrived. Most walked a mile or more when weather permitted. The kindergarten student was usually delivered and picked up by a father who had a problem with alcohol except during the Lenten fasting period. The children were respectful and their parents were very supportive of my efforts. Not all efforts at correcting grammar were completely successful, however. The two children from Tennessee were particularly fond of using "et" instead of eat, ate or have eaten, but we understood them.

The students, whose families were evenly divided between Catholic and Protestant, and supporters of the district, once honored me with a surprise birthday party. Their gift to me was a King James translation of the Bible, with my name inscribed in gold. I was touched by this display of respect and for the evidence of their ethical standards and community unity.

As the year progressed, family health matters and another offer to teach closer to home arose. I knew it would be difficult to leave the love, admiration, and dedication of this first educational adventure.

Patrick, the little kindergartener, and I were swinging on the playground swings as he waited for his ride. He told me he was sad that I wouldn't be his teacher next year. I said I too was sorry, but joked, "Wouldn't it be nice if you could come along with me?"

"Yes," he replied matter-of-factly. "But I don't have a suitcase, so I'll have to stay with Mommy and Daddy."

As pioneering as that first assignment seems to be from the time distance now, and with additional experience in Nebraska rural schools, I can't help but wonder where the educational sphere seems to have gone. Little respect is currently shown for teachers, either by students or their parents. My personal preference would be to still have the one-room school, with the unity of parents and community enriching the lives of the students.

Rev. Francis W. Mennenga grew up on a farm and in the rural community of Wilcox, Nebraska. After teaching at elementary schools in Nebraska and serving in the US Army from 1952 to 1954, he broadened his teaching area to all ages. He graduated from Concordia Theological Seminary, then pastored Lutheran congregations in Hartley, Iowa, and in Texas. In retirement he and his wife live in the Waco suburb of Hewitt.

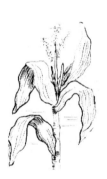

Photo provided by Ronda **Armstrong**

A KINDERGARTEN TALE:
THE CLOWN WHO COULD

Ronda Armstrong

I raced out of the garden ahead of my mom, through the back porch, across the kitchen, and skidded to a stop in front of the calendar on the wall. Just as she caught up with me I spun around to face her.

"How many more days, Mom?"

"Let's count," she said.

We counted, "One. . . two. . . three. . . ," until we reached the date circled in red, the first day of school in Emporia, Kansas.

"I can't wait, Mom!"

She smiled and held my hands while I jumped up and down. After she caught my eye she said, "You'll be a big kindergartener!"

I coped in familiar environments with people I knew. By reading lips I could decipher the gist of the conversation. When I started kindergarten I'd be leaving our safe family cocoon.

It was August 1956. In between Mom's household tasks, garden chores and preparations to send my sister to college, we shopped for school supplies. My enthusiasm about kindergarten grew with the rising stash: crayons, pencils, paper, paints, scissors, and nap mat.

One day we picked out a pattern and fabric for Mom to sew my first-day-of-school dress. Before the big day she snapped a photo of me modeling the brown-and-white gingham checked dress with my new socks and polished shoes. I looked like any other smiling little girl as I posed in front of the low white fence hemming the flower bed on the east side of our house. My bouncing brown hair, freshly permed, covered my ear deformity.

To channel my excitement about school, I gathered miscellaneous pieces of paper from my parents' desk, along with my blackboard, chalk and favorite storyboards, to stock the "school corner" in my room. I lined up my assortment of dolls and stuffed animals, and my cat, Rusty, to act as my students. Rusty soon scampered off, but I spent hours teaching the others at my play school.

Every day I pretended to read to my captive students a book I knew by heart, *The Little Engine That Could*, by Watty Piper. When I corralled my neighborhood playmates, we took turns as teacher. And when the tantalizing smell of my mom's melt-in-your-mouth chocolate chip cookies drifted into the room, the teacher of the day announced, "Children, time to clean up for snacks!"

Those days, until the route became familiar, kids walked to school with classmates, older siblings, or under the watchful eyes of moms stationed along the way. During bad weather parents carpooled.

One evening, after the sun had lowered in the sky and the air cooled, mom and I strolled to Mary Herbert Elementary, the school I would attend a half-mile from our home. I kept up with my mom, who walked with a hitch in her gait and sometimes with a cane, but still, at age four—I wouldn't turn five until late October—it seemed a long walk. After several nights of making this practice trip, I stopped in the last block before we reached home.

"What?" Mom said.

I looked up. "I think I'll need a car!"

I thought my request made perfect sense. Everyone in the family had a vehicle. My father went to work in his trademark fire-engine-red pickup. My mother drove the family car, a two-tone blue Buick. My sister had a sea-green Studebaker. Now that I was starting kindergarten I had a place to go, so why not a car for me too?

I didn't get a car, of course, not for another eleven years. But my mother landed lots of laughs from that story. I'd need the humor to tackle some tough tasks.

The one thing I knew for certain was that I'd love my teacher, Hilda Jones. She was my mom's best friend. They'd grown up together in the country near Overbrook, Kansas, and both had ended up in Emporia. When Mrs. Jones' husband died she returned to college to earn her teaching degree. Who could be better as my first teacher?

On the first day of kindergarten I met more than thirty kids my own age. Keeping track of who said what challenged me. There was much to absorb: an unfamiliar, stimulating environment, directions about lessons and projects, and taking turns with my peers. Before long I figured out that most students knew what to do sooner than I did. My classmates noticed that Mrs. Jones positioned me close to her, or checked with me to be sure I caught instructions. She encouraged all of us to be good helpers and good partners.

Soon the other students followed Mrs. Jones' lead, saying, "Rhonda, come sit by me!" I learned I could count on them to help me, and I did my part by using my astute observation skills.

Mrs. Jones expected me to keep up, but she also gave visual clues and repeated instructions for me.

As the newness of kindergarten wore off, I hounded my mother about Halloween. I wanted to be a clown like the one that rode on the engine in *The Little Engine That Could*. I liked the upbeat clown in the story, who persisted until a willing engine agreed to pull the stranded load of toys over the mountain. As a youngster who couldn't hear or talk like other kids, I identified with the little blue engine that struggled to scale the mountain. The clown in that story didn't give up. Neither did the determined blue engine. Neither did I.

My mom made a red-and-white-checked clown suit for me. We found a jolly clown mask to complete the costume. I practiced saying, "Hello, I'm Ronda the Clown!" But with the mask my words sounded garbled, and the "r" was a hard sound for me to produce. Sometimes I left out the "l" in clown, a sound I didn't always hear correctly.

In April of my kindergarten year, I had my first ear surgery at St. Luke's Hospital in Kansas City. Since my birth the doctors had wondered if I had a left ear under the flap of skin. As it turned out, I didn't. Complex surgery created a canal to the inner ear, and an outer ear was shaped.

I began to understand the differences in my life. Other kids didn't stay in antiseptic-smelling hospitals, nor did they wake up with shells covering new, makeshift ears, or have bandages wrapping their heads.

Mrs. Jones kept me connected to school. She sent me copies of the books the class was reading, with suggestions for projects

I could do. She visited me while I recuperated. My classmates mailed cards and drawings.

My parents and Mrs. Jones grasped what I didn't yet understand, which was that I had a permanent hearing loss that would stay with me through my school years and adult life.

Before the end of the school year, I returned to kindergarten, eager to delve in. Quiet but determined, I relied on my natural curiosity, observation skills and my desire to be a part of the group. I'd already learned that I could count on my classmates and the adults around me to give me relevant clues. I could handle the rest.

My teacher supported my efforts and focused on my strengths. She summarized my progress for my parents. "Ronda has made splendid progress this year in spite of her handicap. She is so alert that she is able to follow group activity and miss very little. She is dependable and accepts responsibility. She has varied interests. She especially enjoys books, and loves stories and pictures. She finds things that will interest other children and is well liked by them."

Reminiscent of my favorite story, when I mastered a task my mother would say, "I thought you could!"

Kindergarten gave me the foundation I needed to navigate the school years ahead of me. I discovered that I could be resourceful and chug up the mountain on my own steam, optimistic and undaunted. I was no longer the clown who had masqueraded for Halloween; I was the clown who could.

I kept my "I can" spirit and my enthusiasm for learning. Years later I became a school social worker, helping families and teachers empower students with different needs.

When students become their own problem solvers, they sustain themselves over life's long haul, just like the clown in the story who persisted, with the little blue engine, to carry a load of toys over the mountain.

Ronda Armstrong lives with her husband and two cats in Iowa. Her recent work has appeared in *Chicken Soup for the Soul* and *The Des Moines Register*. When not writing she reads, dances, and connects with family and friends.

Photo provided by Joneva Anderson Currans

OLD DOG

Joneva Anderson Currans

For some reason, we never got around to naming him. He was called Pup until his muzzle turned gray and then he became Old Dog. He didn't bond with us humans like others of his species. There was no tongue-lolling, or dancing on hind legs with joy when we came home from school.

"Here, Pup," we'd call. "Come here, come here!"

He'd look over his shoulder and keep on going.

We'd try again. "Come back here!"

By that time he'd be out of sight.

When electricity came to the farm a crew of young men wired the buildings and did all that was needed to bring us into the modern world of light and labor-saving devices. Old Dog was sleeping soundly in the sunshine when the REA truck drove into the yard. Being young men of humor, they drove their truck carefully, tires straddling the sleeping dog, and parked it there. They meant no harm, but the temptation was too great.

Old Dog awoke to find himself surrounded by four tires and the greasy undercarriage of the vehicle. From then on he was a changed canine. His duty in life became to make sure anything resembling a truck or car was chased speedily away from his home territory.

My folks lived on a farm next to the highway. Old Dog lurked among the tall ditch grasses until he heard the sound of an approaching motor. Then he came roaring up out of the ditch, barking madly, to chase the offending car or pickup until he was sure it was well on its way to Graettinger or Emmetsburg.

Sometimes he misjudged the speed or intent of the driver and was tumbled tail-over-teacup back to where he'd come from. When this happened he limped back up the driveway to sulk under the lilac bushes.

My mother felt sorry for him and brought out a dish of scraps and some cool water. Old Dog didn't ignore her. She brought food. After nursing his sore feelings for a while he scratched at the screen door until he got his nose in and slipped inside to lie on the wooden cellar door. It was hard for him to get comfortable, however. He sighed, groaned and scratched his various itchy spots. His hind leg thumped on the cellar door.

Sigh, groan, *thump- thump- thump.* Over and over.

Finally, Mom could stand it no longer. "*Gå och laga,*" she'd say to him. "*Gå och laga, så att lusa fa mat!*"*

Old Dog stared at her perplexedly, one ear up and one ear down. He had difficulties with English, let alone Mom's particular brand of Swedish.

Slowly comprehension dawned in his doggy brain. She must mean cars were coming to attack!

He struggled to his feet, dived through the bottom quadrant of the screen door, kicked himself loose from its grip on his hind quarters and ran as fast as he could, barking wildly, ready to take on anything with wheels and an engine. Maybe, even a semi.

Old Dog would save Mom, the farm and everything else in his domain!

*My Grandpa Swenson was a Swedish immigrant and we often heard bits and phrases of that language in our home. My mother would never tell me what "*gå laga*" meant and I was sure it was something too awful to hear. Eventually she confessed it meant, "Go lay down so the lice can get something to eat."

Joneva Anderson Currans has always enjoyed words, both in reading and writing them. Her goal is to share her memories and experiences with the next generation. When her children were young they thought she'd lived in the pioneer days. She wants her grandchildren to know that she arrived long after the dinosaurs.

Photo provided by Carolyn Rohrbaugh

SQUEAKY AND ME

Carolyn Rohrbaugh

I didn't realize until long into my life what a wonderful thing it was to grow up in small-town Iowa in the 1940s and '50s. My town was and still is Sutherland.

As I look back, I don't think there were many rich people living in Sutherland at the time. We all worked hard, kids included, and neighbors were always there to help. I didn't realize that if we were rich we would have had a bathroom in the house, store-bought canned goods, store-bought clothes and a car to go out of town shopping.

Dad had many jobs. Most people did, as there were no manufacturing companies around. He owned an upholstery shop where he fixed canvases for windrowers and upholstered furniture. Later he sold Norge appliances and Emerson televisions. He ran the projector at the theater, tilled gardens, drove the school bus and was a night watchman. My sister Darla Rae and I were always required to help with the chores.

Sunday was church day. When we finally got a car, when I was six or seven, we could visit our aunts and uncles in Paullina and Primghar.

Monday was wash day. We would pump water from the hand pump to fill the copper boiler. Mother had a gas hotplate on the back porch for heating the water to be transferred to the wringer washer. All clothes were washed in the same water, so it was important to sort the loads by color, starting with the whites. The clothes were hung outside year 'round. Darla Rae and I were glad we had school so we didn't have to hang clothes out in the winter, but we were required to bring them in after school. If they hadn't frozen dry we'd hang them on a clothes rack in the house.

Each day had several chores: washing, ironing, cleaning, baking, gardening, canning, mowing, and feeding the chickens

and rabbits. We had animals in town, as there were no ordin-
ances back then prohibiting it.

It seems we had many chores, but we still had plenty of time
to play. Patty and Mike Steuermann lived down the street. We all
loved to play house, as well as guns and cowboys.

Mrs. Mangels, a widow lady with grown children, lived across
the street. Each morning she would be either working in her
garden or mowing her yard with her reel-type mower. It was a
push mower, with no motor. At coffee time she would cross the
street to our house. I always watched for her. She would scrape
the garden dirt from her shoes as she came up the sidewalk,
scraping and whistling a tune. As she approached the back door
she didn't knock, just called "Yoo-hoo!" as she stepped in.

I always hurried to beat Mother to greet her. One day Mrs.
Mangels had a few of her daughter's dresses draped over her
arm. She gave them to me, saying I could have them to play
dress-up in. My eyes were firmly set on a green taffeta dress that
looked fit for a queen. Usually Darla Rae got what she wanted
first, so I had to move quickly. One leap and I had that dress. No
one had to tell me a second time to take my pick.

After that my thoughts turned to the storage shed attached to
our garage. It would be a wonderful playhouse and a place to
keep my dress. Mother must have given it some thought too, and
we were soon cleaning out the shed. Mother had an apple crate
that was divided in the center. She set the crate on end, made
curtains, and we had a kitchen cupboard in the playhouse. Ada
Heckert, who lived next door, brought over some old dishes and
pots and pans.

We spent hours in that playhouse. I was pretty selfish about
my beautiful green dress. My friend Kary Steuck lived two
houses down and had an older sister. Kary's sister not only gave
her dresses, but also high-heeled platform shoes. I liked to wear
the shoes but the trade-off was that I had to let Kary wear my
dress.

One day Mrs. Mangels told us to come over, she had some of
her daughter's shoes to give us. I couldn't believe it when I saw a
pair of high-heeled platform shoes, which meant I wouldn't have
to share my dress with Kary.

Life seemed to be going along great when, early one morning,
I ran outside to sit in the warm sun. There on the porch was an

old yellow dog with a partially healed gunshot wound to his hip. He didn't bark, he just squeaked. We looked into each other's eyes and a love instantly formed between us.

I yelled to Mother to come quick. "Can I have him, Mother, can I have him?" I begged.

She looked the dog over and said his wound was well on the way to being healed. And yes, I could keep him.

Through the years Squeaky and I were inseparable. I can't begin to tell you how many dresses he was dressed up in, including my valuable green taffeta dress. I pulled him around in the wagon, but when we played guns he would disappear.

Squeaky was always there to greet me after school or whenever we left and returned, and always with that special *squeak-squeak-squeak* and a wagging tail until I grabbed him and gave him a hug.

I've always liked to get up early. My favorite place to go as the sun came up was the sidewalk in front of the house. It was quiet and warm sitting in the early morning sun. Sometimes I'd draw pictures on the sidewalk with my chalk. Squeaky always joined me. He was so smart that I decided to teach him to talk. We completely understood each other, and I couldn't believe others didn't understand him. Next I decided he must learn to write. I would push the chalk between his toes and guide his leg through the ABCs, then his name and then mine.

"See, Mother, he can write."

When I was eight years old our brother Jim was born, and when I was ten our sister Paula was born. Babysitting was another chore added to the list. Squeaky became a very good babysitter. Several grandparents around town had their grandchildren visiting during the summer, and most of them loved to come to our playhouse. One afternoon Mother told Darla Rae and me we would have to stay home and watch baby Jim. Soon after Mother left, the Hughes' grandchildren came over to play, so Darla Rae and I put Jim down for a nap and we played in the playhouse. When it was time for the Hughes' grandkids to leave we walked with them. We walked and played and completely forgot we were supposed to be babysitting. When we got home later we were met by an angry mother.

Our Grandma and Grandpa Silberstein, as well as aunts, uncles and cousins, all lived in Russell, Minnesota. Darla Rae and I would go there and spend a week or so each summer. Our cousins, Helen and Marlene, had all the latest toys, things I had never seen before. They had actual dish cupboards, tables and chairs, kid-sized pastel glass dishes and a tin Ferris wheel that really went around.

When our parents came to pick us up after one of these visits all thirty-some of the relatives would get together for one of the happiest reunions ever. Grandpa and Grandma lived on a f arm and all of us kids would run to the creek to play for hours on end. Every Fourth of July Uncle Delton brought a watermelon and would put it in the clear, clean water to cool. But after a week of fun and happiness, the best thing of all was to get home to Squeaky, squeaking and wagging his tail. We were always so happy to see each other.

One summer weekend when I was eleven our parents took us to Russell for a week's visit. Before leaving I hugged Squeaky and told him I'd see him next weekend. We always had fun at Russell. That is where we had our first soft ice cream cones, called whirl-a-whips.

The week flew by and I was especially anxious to go home. I missed Squeaky and was glad to see my parents, but I could tell something was wrong. They took me aside and told me Squeaky had gotten sick and they'd had to put him to sleep.

I cried and cried, for the rest of the weekend and all the way home.

To this day I have so many questions. But I waited too long to ask my parents about it, and when I did they couldn't remember, or perhaps they didn't want to. Squeaky was fine when I left. How did he get sick so quickly? It's something I'll wonder about forever. I've had many beloved pets throughout my life but that dog was the most special of all. Squeaky taught me about love, respect, trust and most of all unselfishness. What a special part of my life he was.

Carolyn (Gottsch) Rohrbaugh and her husband Bill live in Sutherland, Iowa, where she's been on the city council and is now the mayor. They have two children and five grandchildren. She loves a challenge and enjoys writing, especially poetry.

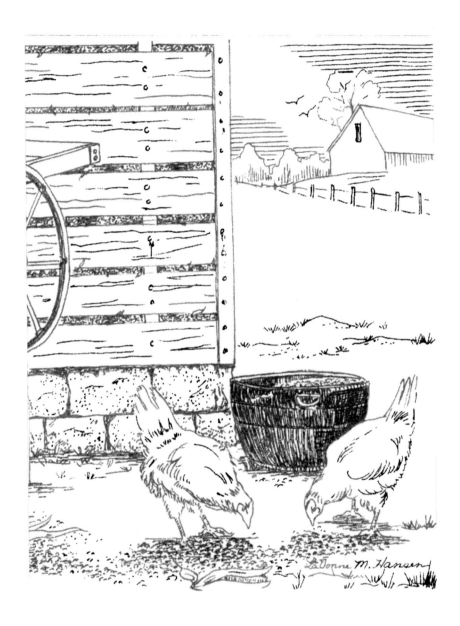

Drawing by LaVonne M. Hansen

GARDEN OF NO RETURN

Jd Schooley

There was a time when sitting and whittling on a stick was just a way to pass time for small-town America. For old Tony and me, we did that on a daily basis. I was four years old and Tony was eighty-one years my senior. He had the curmudgeon thing in spades and in between long deep gasps for air, he let out irregular long guttural exhalations, intended to shock and scare off any who might have achieved even a minor level of comfort in his outdoor domain. It worked well on newcomers, the faint of heart and any unsuspecting crows that had recently landed in his garden.

"Ah. . . whee. . . *phaaaw!*" and then he'd spit, right at your foot if he was of a mind.

Tony was tall and lean, and he carried a hefty cane that he enjoyed thumping loudly near his chair. Then he would go back to his morning coffee while listening to the farm report coming from the bakelite radio in his musty old garage.

The air was sweet with apple blossoms, the wind drifted through his collection of fishing lures, dangling above his carving bench. I was amazed. Amazed by an old man who'd out-lived the horse and plow but refused to stop being a farmer, even right in the middle of town. I was amazed that he had such a large garden and kept chickens too.

We had just moved in next door, filling the little house with my folks, three sisters, an older brother, a new baby brother and one dog, Lady. Named for the dog in "Lady and the Tramp," the Disney movie, our Lady looked nothing like the one in the film. Our Lady was a big golden Labrador retriever. She had not turned out to be the hunting dog my dad had envisioned. She was a gun coward, and was resigned to being the family pet.

While I waited for my siblings to return home from school, we spent the long days together, Lady and me and old Tony.

Each morning started with us seated below the shady apple tree, surveying the garden within its tall fence. The radio in the garage would sing out the latest market reports. Tony whittled and painted his fishing lures between occasional weeding. I retrieved the morning paper from where it arrived on the drive with a loud thump. Lady would roll in the dirt, nipping at flies while Tony's wife brought tall glasses of lemonade from the kitchen. Life was good.

Though Tony tolerated my stories and answered all my millions of questions with his routine loud *"Phaaaw!"* he would have preferred to be shed of me, had it not been for Tony's wife. Her kind words had him at a loss to do anything but sit and wait for me to go home for lunch or my nap so he could cuss and spit with impunity.

Tony's garden had a ten-foot-tall fence that circled the potatoes, melons, sweet corn and such. Two reasons required such great height—retaining chickens, which he sheltered in a hut behind the old garage, and restricting baseballs. The chickens kept insects off his plants and added a fertilizing agent to his wonderful crop. The balls came in on a regular basis by way of the adjacent Catholic school playground that nearly surrounded Tony's garden.

The hens were shielded from view by a thick-leafed grapevine from which Tony managed to obtain fairly large grapes. I doubt I tasted even one of those grapes, since he was a fierce guardian of his domain and all it contained. Paramount to this protection was the errant pop fly. Whenever one of the baseballs got over his fence, landing in the orderly rows of tomato and cucumber vines, he would slowly shuffle his long tall frame over to the substantial gate. Once through the gate he steadied his way down the wide plank walkway with a long-handled spade. He paid no attention to the eyes belonging to the fingers clinched all along the wire enclosure, awaiting his response. Then with his spade he would calmly roll the ball to a suitable spot and proceed to put it deep into the soft loam as the compost he judged it to be.

Only one gutsy student had ever clambered over the fence to save his ball from the garden of no return. The Kepler boy got the ball and tossed it back to the others, but paid for his transgression by way of a swat on the behind from a long-handled spade before he could launch himself back over the fence. He made history, but none had the nerve to repeat his achievement.

From our house it was only a block to the Farm Co-op Elevator. At this wonderful place, area farmers would bring their wagonloads of feed corn and such over the big scale built into the drive there. Once the total weight was known, the load would be removed and the return weight balanced out to determine what had been the product weight. As all the different trucks of farm produce came and went, Lady noted with great interest that some of the trucks contained crates of highly prized fowl—chickens! They were stacked high and wide in crates that fit together and had swing gates that allowed the birds to be placed inside and, when appropriate, removed. By and by a gate would become dislodged, or a desperate hen of great genius would manage its escape. Lady, being the natural bird dog she was, saw her opportunity, would catch the escapee and proudly make her way home.

First to take notice was old Tony. He quickly made it his business to emancipate the poor droopy fowl, and then deliver it to his chicken hutch for safe keeping. Eventually the teamwork became so efficient with this operation that Tony had only to take count to gain a new occupant. The spring-loaded gate allowed Lady to make a deposit to the pen night or day. Tony was elated. Lady wouldn't tell. All she desired was an atta-girl and a pat on the head.

By the end of summer, Tony's chicken population had blossomed into a veritable explosion of white, fat, egg-laying, bug-picking fertilizers. Lady was a champion in Tony's eyes.

One Sunday morning the boys from the elevator came over during the after-church glad-handing session and asked my dad if he didn't have a big yellow lab. Proud of the dog, Dad gleefully admitted to owning such a bird dog.

"You haven't noticed her showing up with a chicken now and then?" they asked. Then all participated in a lot of head-scratching as Dad denied gaining any hens that way.

"I'll keep an eye on her," was his reply.

Of course, my dad knew nothing about it, but on the way home he peeked through the grape vines.

"Sure enough," he told Mom, "half of Tony's hens have no feathers on their necks."

"Well you don't know how they got there, so best say nothing and keep the dog in during business hours," she suggested.

No matter, Lady would sniff out any breakouts, whatever the hour. She and Tony continued to carry on like a couple of pros. She got the praise, he got the eggs and regular fried chicken on his plate, and I enjoyed the big red apples that bounced onto the shady lawn by Tony's garage. I was an unsuspecting partner in crime, but relished in the rewards for supplying the getaway device. We were a crime ring of an unusual mix.

Soon the kids returned to school and the balls again landed in the garden. This fall was different. The Kepler boy had noticed how the arrangement was working with Tony and my dog, and whenever he got a chance he would play toss-the-ball with Lady. He would then give her pieces of his lunch. As soon as the noon whistle sounded, she was off to play with the kids.

The next time a ball landed in the garden, Lady was at the ready. When Tony loosened the latch on the gate, she pushed past him and bounded right through the hanging vines. Grabbing the ball in her teeth, she raced back to the ball field for a reward of peanut butter sandwich.

Old Tony was furious. "Phaaaaw!" he bellowed. "That darned no-good dog!" He threw down his shovel and shuffled back to his chair to sulk. When Lady returned he was abusive toward her and made target of her with spit.

Soon this routine became the norm. No matter how Tony tried to exclude Lady from the garden, she always managed to retrieve the balls. With this change in loyalty she lost favor in Tony's eye and he set about to give her a poke with his cane if he could. He turned off the radio, removed all the apples and spent recess time indoors. Lady, however, was industrious, and the next morning he found the gate standing open. All over the garden were small mounds of dirt, each with a corresponding hole. The balls Tony had previously buried lay piled upon home plate.

A new alliance had developed and the kids made friends with Lady. She would spend all the recess time running after the kids and rescuing their balls.

Finally, Tony'd had enough. That fall when all the produce was harvested from the garden, he propped the gate open and tied a stout rope onto it. "Here you go, Lady!" he said and tossed a big apple into the garden. Lady bounded after it, and when she was well inside the fence, he pulled the rope, shutting the gate tight. Next he tied the rope securely and, chuckling gleefully, went inside for dinner.

Lady sat and waited by the gate. She expected some reward. Tony went to bed, and Lady waited patiently late into the night. When it grew cold, Lady decided she had had enough.

In the morning Tony woke up and went to the window to look out at his clever trick and see what had transpired. What he saw was a big hole under his gate.

"Phaaah!" Tony shouted. He hurried down the stairs in his bathrobe, past the fresh coffee and the morning paper. Out the back door he bitterly shuffled toward his ruined garden gate. Then he stopped short halfway across the yard. What he saw made him speechless. The door to the chicken hutch was standing open and all his chickens were gone. Lady sat proudly by the apple tree waiting for the morning farm report.

That Sunday morning I overheard the boys from the elevator say, "You wouldn't know about that golden lab that brung us all those twenty-some chickens last week? That's some bird dog!"

Soon our parents bought their first house and we moved to the other side of town. Lady went to live with friends who had a farm with lots of dog-friendly space. I attended the school where Tony and his garden partook of the warm sunny afternoons next to the playground of noisy, ball-chasing children. I never sat with Tony again, nor did I enjoy the fruit of his garden and the glorious red apples. For Lady and me, Tony's world had become, truly, a garden of no return.

Jd Schooley creates his stories and poems in the place of his childhood, along the banks of the Little Sioux River in northwest Iowa. As an artist he also sculpts wood, acts and directs for theater and restores antiques. He can be found most days at his downtown Spencer studio/coffee shop, Toad's, where he gratefully signs copies of this book.

Photo provided by Marilyn Wells

THERE'S A HORSE ON THE PORCH!

Marilyn Wells

From the time I was five or so, all I could think of was how to get a horse. Even though we had no place to keep a horse, every year I was just certain that Santa would bring me one.

But when I was eleven, my family moved to a house in the town of Marathon that had belonged to my great-grandfather. It had a large pasture and a barn—just the place to keep a horse! Finally, when I was thirteen, my parents relented and said I could get one. We scoured the want ads until we found what we were looking for—a two year old, part Arabian filly, "green broke," which meant she was accustomed to a bridle and had been ridden a few times. She was on a farm by Royal. She cost one hundred dollars, which Mom and Dad had very generously given me to buy her.

She looked rather ungainly, with her head a bit too large for her body, and what was called a "glass eye"—one that had a blue iris instead of the usual brown, while the other one was normal. She was what's known as a "white pinto," mostly white, with a few black spots. To me she was beautiful. I named her Chita.

I got Chita in February of that year, which was fortunate, because there was still snow on the ground. This made falling off much less painful, and I fell off a lot at first. My dad decided I should ride bareback for the first year to gain a sense of balance on the horse. Riding bareback wasn't so bad during the winter, when it was cold and I was wearing thick jeans anyway, but once the weather warmed up, riding for even short periods of time left my legs and seat covered with a layer of sweaty, prickly horse-hair.

That first summer I tried several devices that weren't exactly saddles, but did provide a little distance between me and my steed. The first was simply a saddle blanket with a cinch belt around it, but as soon as the horse moved, the blanket and I slid right off. Next I tried a canvas contraption that looked like an

English saddle. It at least had stirrups, but they rested so close to the horse that I couldn't get my feet into them, so that was pretty useless too.

When my year of bareback riding was up I could finally get a real saddle. Saddles were expensive, however, and my funds were very limited.

I had just taken over the newspaper route for *The Sioux City Journal* from my brother. I had to pick up the papers by six a.m. and have them delivered in time to get home, cleaned up, dressed for school and at my desk in the high school by eight. The only transportation I had for this task was a heavy old bicycle that took most of the energy I had just to get it moving. By the time I loaded it with papers and pedaled it all over town, I was exhausted. If I just had a saddle, I reasoned, I could use Chita to deliver the papers and get home and to school with time to spare.

But how was I going to get a saddle that I didn't have the money to buy? I'd have to borrow the funds from someone, but whom? I didn't want to ask my parents because they simply couldn't afford it. There was one other possibility—the bank.

Earlier that year, in my role as assistant editor for the high school newspaper, I had met and interviewed Mr. Norris Olney, president of the Marathon State bank, for an article I was writing about the town park. Mr. Olney took great pride in the park's appearance, and often helped with the upkeep himself. He was a dignified older gentleman, someone I would not ordinarily even feel comfortable speaking to, much less asking for a loan, but at the time he had seemed genuinely pleased to be interviewed. He had also mentioned that he knew my father, grandfather, and even my great-grandfather.

Figuring I had nothing to lose by asking, I screwed up my courage and walked into Mr. Olney's office to ask for a loan. I explained that I had a steady job delivering newspapers and needed the saddle so I could deliver them faster by horseback. This would leave more time available for expanding my route and making more money.

I guess this sounded plausible to him, because he agreed to give me a loan for fifty dollars, the amount I had requested. He said that since he'd known my family for so long, I wouldn't need any collateral. He then took me out to the front of the bank and introduced me to Mr. Ralph Hartley, the head cashier, who helped me open a checking account for my loan money.

With the loan check safely deposited, I set about finding just the right saddle. It took a while, but I finally settled on a beautiful black one with a red padded seat and covered stirrups.

The day it arrived I could hardly contain my excitement as Dad helped me open the huge box. He helped me carry it to the barn and made sure I knew how to set it on Chita and get all the buckles buckled and the straps latched. Then I was off, around the pasture on my new saddle, getting used to the feel of it as Chita got used to the idea of something new and heavy on her back.

It was time to try the saddle out for real. I got up early to make sure everything was in order, then saddled Chita up and walked her the two blocks to the post office, where the newspapers came in every morning. I loaded the papers into the canvas delivery bag, draped the strap over my saddle horn and started off on my maiden voyage.

The route went beautifully. Chita walked carefully up to each doorway I took her to, and stopped while I leaned over and dropped the newspaper in the proper place. We developed a rhythm, working together efficiently.

Only one more stop and then we would head for home and breakfast.

I'd deliberately left the Bockelman house for last because it would require me to dismount to get the paper inside the front door, which was in the middle of a low porch.

I trailed the long reins in my hand as I approached the Bockelmans' screen door, opened it, dropped the paper and turned to leave, when much to my astonishment, there came Chita up the two steps and onto the porch! Hoping no one had heard the heavy clomp of hooves on the wooden porch, I turned Chita toward the steps and pulled on the reins to get her down as fast as I could. But she didn't want to go.

When a horse won't go straight ahead, it will sometimes move if you turn the head as if to change direction or turn all the way around and then start off in the same direction you wanted to go. I tried this several times, but to no avail. All this tugging and turning resulted in much more clomping noise on the porch.

Desperation was starting to set in. As horses often do when they are stressed, Chita lifted her tail and deposited a steaming pile of "road apples" on the porch. By that time, there had been so much noise on the wood porch that several members of the Bockelman family had come to look out the front windows to see what was going on.

"Mom!" a small voice yelled. "There's a horse on the porch!"

Bob was the first to come dashing out the door. He was the one I'd dreaded seeing most. A senior in high school, he had little time for a freshman like me. And he looked angry.

"What the heck is going on out here?" he demanded. "You get that thing out of here and get that mess cleaned up!"

I started to tell him I was trying to, but he had already slammed the front door shut.

I continued trying to get Chita off the porch. When my attempts failed, I worked up all the courage I could muster and timidly knocked on the door. Much to my relief, it was answered by Mrs. Bockelman, a gentle-looking lady. I barely knew her, but I was very thankful to see her.

"Mrs. Bockelman, may I please use your phone to call my folks?" I asked.

"Sure, dear. Come right in. It's over there on the wall," she said, gesturing.

I quickly dialed our number and was relieved when my mother answered.

"Mom?" I said, my voice quivering, "I'm at Bockelman's, and I was just delivering the paper when Chita climbed up on their porch and pooped on it, and now I can't get her down." I sobbed quietly. "What am I going to do?"

"She did what?" Mom asked, sounding incredulous. "How in heaven's name did that happen?"

I explained the situation as best I could, trying to keep an eye on Chita as I spoke. I'd left the reins tied to the post that held up the porch roof, and I was hoping she wouldn't take off and pull the porch post down with her.

"Well, I suppose you could try coming back here and getting a pail with some corn in it and rattle it around to see if she'll follow it," Mom suggested. "And take a shovel!"

"Okay," I whispered. "I'll be there in a minute."

I'd lost so much time already that I was in danger of being late for school.

I thanked Mrs. Bockelman and headed out the door, intent on running the six blocks to home and back as fast as I could. But, much to my absolute horror, I saw Mr. Hartley, the head cashier at the bank and the Bockelman's next door neighbor, come dashing out of his front door. He was wearing his pajamas, an old bathrobe, and huge unbuckled galoshes as he stomped through the snow. He wielded a large household broom in his hands. Within seconds he was up on the porch, and with a mighty swing of the broom he whacked Chita across the rear end, sending her leaping off the porch.

Fortunately, I had the reins in my hand by then or the porch roof post would have gone with her. I was dragged along behind her, but was able to gain control of her head as she started to take off, and finally managed to pull her to a stop.

I yelled my thanks to Mr. Hartley as I took off at a run, Chita trotting beside me. I would have to return after school to clean up the porch. As I ran I vowed I would never, ever do *that* again!

To this day I inwardly cringe as I remember walking to the Bockelmans' house after school with a snow shovel and a bucket to clean up the mess my dear horse had left on their porch. This was something a high school girl simply should not have to do.

I still had a beautiful saddle, but with no way to pay for it other than to get out my old bicycle every morning and slowly pedal my way around the little town. I finished each morning exhausted, but comforted myself with the knowledge that I was building character as well as muscle mass. It took another six months of delivering papers to get the saddle paid for, but the day finally came when I made the last payment to the bank and joyfully handed the route over to a neighbor boy, feeling a great sense of relief that I no longer had to rise at the break of dawn.

And so ended my brief and inglorious career as a horse-riding papergirl.

Marilyn Wells grew up in Marathon, Iowa. She is a retired physician who lives in Phoenix. From 1992-2000 she enjoyed her position as one of the team doctors for the Phoenix Suns. Health issues now limit her activities, but she enjoys reading, writing, public television and doing research on the Internet.

Photo provided by **Marjorie Dohlman**

SUMMERS SPENT HORSIN' AROUND

Marjorie Dohlman

An adventurous kid who grows up on a farm learns many life lessons such as compassion, patience, responsibility and the need for hard work. The hard work of farm life also gives a person a strong appreciation for the occasional free time that comes his or her way. As I grew up, summers were a great time for me since this was the time of year when farm chores were a little less time-consuming and allowed for my favorite pastime of riding a horse.

Hardly a summer day went by without at least one of my siblings or me riding one of the horses in our menagerie. The ragtag bunch included a bay mare named Pixie; a black gelding called Lightning; Princess, the dappled mini-pony; Smokey, a leggy Arabian; a burly plug called Squirt; and Birdie, a cantankerous roan pony.

Birdie was the one I rode most often. I'm not quite sure how the family pecking order of who rode what left me as the unlucky one to ride Birdie. I suspect it had something to do with the fact that, at the time, I may well have been just as stubborn as that pony. Now don't get me wrong, Birdie wasn't all bad. I'm sure she must have had some redeeming qualities. I just can't seem to think of them right now. But Birdie wasn't the only horse on the farm who gave me some of the more wild summer rides horsin' around.

Our laid-back bay mare, Pixie, with the help of my mischievous brothers, gave me the fastest ride of my life. Of course my perception of the speed may have been tainted. After all, it was hard to gauge the actual speed when I couldn't see where I was going. My temporary blindness was due to the fact that my brother had pulled my hat down over my eyes and given Pixie a jolting swat on the rump. Pixie took off like a shot and continued at a rapid pace that was egged on by my screams. I guess she thought I was screaming, "Go, go," when I was actually screaming, "Whoa, whoa!" It was all I could do to keep one hand in a death-grip on her mane and the other clinging tightly to the reins.

Lightning, the black gelding, gave me my first experience as a bronc rider. I was taking him out on his first spring ride after a long winter's rest, when suddenly I was six inches off the saddle, then twelve inches, and then I was whipped forward over his neck as he gave one final kick that sent his heels toward the sun. Luckily, I was able to keep a white-fisted grip on the saddle horn and my feet firmly in the stirrups so I didn't sail ten feet into the air. I still cringe when I think of how hard that landing would have been.

Lightning was also my companion on one of my trips to bring the cows in for milking. On that particular day the cows decided the place they wanted to be was at the far corner of a hilly pasture where the paths were steep and rocky. Lightning and I were on our way up a path when he stumbled on a rock. I was riding bareback and started sliding toward his rump as he worked to regain his footing. I grabbed for his neck and wrapped my arms tightly around it as he stabilized himself and finally made his way up the rest of the hill. By the time we got to the top, I was lying flat along his back with my toes dangling over his rump. Needless to say, on the way home Lightning and I followed the cows' lead and took an alternate path that wound more casually around the edge of the hill.

In all of my experiences, Birdie gave me the most adventurous rides. The adventure usually began when it came time to catch her. Birdie definitely had a sixth sense when it came to knowing that someone was headed out to catch her. I learned early that trickery was needed. A pail containing a few kernels of corn or an ear of corn were good Birdie-catching tools. I would shake the corn in the bottom of the bucket and the horses would come over to get some. Birdie stayed at arm's length until the munching of the other horses got the best of her. But her need to have a nibble eventually outweighed her determination not to get caught. That nibble-attempt on her part was my one chance to catch her. When Birdie snitched a lightning-quick bite I had to move fast to get the reins over her neck. If I missed, I'd spend what seemed like hours cornering her.

Once caught, Birdie's cantankerous nature didn't improve. One of her favorite tricks was to run through the back yard to see if she could "clothesline" her rider. She succeeded a time or two. Birdie was also well known for her "walnut tree trick." Whenever Birdie wanted to get rid of a rider, especially an adult rider, she'd head full-force toward the walnut tree in our yard to sideswipe the rider and knock him or her off. I can't even venture a guess as to how many riders ended up with scraped knees, knuckles and elbows at her expense.

Birdie's biggest trick left me once with a half-mile walk home. On that momentous day my two brothers, my sister and I were all riding in the newly-baled hay field. There was a ravine about halfway down the field. This was by no means a big ravine. Even our mini-pony looked like a professional jumper when she hopped over the ravine.

On that particular day, Birdie decided she was not going to jump the ravine. The only problem was she didn't let me know her plan. When we reached the ravine all of the other horses did their usual leap. Not Birdie. She came to a dead stop. I flew forward, dangling precariously over her neck. Birdie was definitely no dumb horse. When I didn't immediately fall off she put her head down to send me sliding toward the ground. I slid right down over her ears, and so did the bridle. When Birdie realized she was free from the bridle she took off for home at breakneck speed. She caught up with, and even passed, my siblings on their horses. All I could do was watch the ensuing dust trail get farther away, gather up my bridle and enjoy my leisurely walk home.

I often think about those fun, character-building times during my childhood summers. Especially when the little bone chip in my elbow gives a quick jolt and reminds me of the day Birdie bucked me off onto the cement steps by our house.

Marjorie Dohlman grew up on a dairy farm in Chatfield, Minnesota. Besides spending time with her daughters, she enjoys reading, writing and listening to music. She now lives in Riceville, Iowa, and still has a horse.

Drawing by LaVonne M. Hansen

THE WAY MY CROW FLIES

Jane Kauzlarich

If you've ever traveled the green, rolling hills and golden plains of Iowa's countryside, you've undoubtedly spotted large flocks of huge black crows congregated in the cornfields, enjoying a veritable feast. To most people, especially Iowa farmers, a crow is just a bothersome bird that robs the fields of precious grain. This sinister-looking creature is considered a thief. It's common practice in Iowa farm country to go hunting for crows, since the raucous bird is considered a pest.

I'm very familiar with the crow. My home is in Northwest Iowa, where they're plentiful. When I was eleven years old my father gave me a pet crow, and I came to realize that the crow is truly an unusual bird.

We adopted our crow when he was very young. He was an ugly little creature. The first time I saw him sitting in Dad's hand he was just a little black blob of messy, fluffed-up feathers. His eyes were half shut, but I later discovered, to my surprise, that his eyes were a beautiful pale blue.

We kept Crowby, as my dad named our unique pet, in the basement in a chicken coop until he was old enough to stay outside all the time. When he was hungry, which was most of the time, his loud "cawing" could be plainly heard all through the house. We fed him little balls of bread dipped in milk, which he relished. Later on, Strongheart canned dog food, also rolled into balls, was his favorite dish.

Many times when he was full and could eat no more, Crowby would hide the remaining balls of dog food, and I'd have to pretend I wasn't watching. He'd use his miraculous beak to stab the precious morsel into the dirt, then, with his comical Charlie Chaplin saunter, he'd grab a leaf and place it over the cache. He had a knack for hiding his treasures.

Besides the dog food, Crowby also ate insects and worms, which he caught himself. Once he devoured my entire butterfly and bee collection, which I'd intended to release after studying them closely for a day or two. Crowby was fat. I imagine that was because he didn't have to work very hard for his food.

Crowby grew up to be a truly beautiful bird. His feathers were shiny black with a glinting purple tint. He had a long, very sharp black beak. His aim with that beak was remarkable. When I tempted him with grass and twigs held between my fingers, he'd rear back and slam his beak at the tidbit I held, never once nicking my skin.

Crowby's beautiful blue eyes were covered with two sets of eyelids. The inner eyelid closed from side to side, and the outer lid closed like ours do. His claws were sharp, and his toes were long and flexible. He liked to ride around on me as I explored our backyard, the fence rows, our raspberry patch and the barn where we kept our banty chickens. With Crowby on my shoulder, we'd cross the field leading to the Milwaukee Railroad tracks, where we examined smoldering logs and empty tin cans left by the hobos who rode the rails and politely thanked my mother for the sandwiches and pieces of angel food cake she gave them.

Crowby spent time on the roof of our back porch, because from that vantage point he could fly from my brother's bedroom window to mine, pecking and chortling and cawing. On occasion I let him into my room.

When I left my little town for Walther League Camp at Lake Okoboji, Dad wrote me post cards: "Crowby has been trying to get into the house. He misses you."

And once, while I was gone, he did get in, flying through the house, cawing and searching for me. I wonder if he knew that I was crying silent tears around the campfire, missing my family and my feathered companion.

Our pet crow was notorious in our town. He had a reputation for stealing bright and glittering objects. He'd peck open the shiny milk bottle caps early in the morning, spilling milk all over our front porch. In those days milk was delivered every day in glass bottles. Many of the things Crowby did were funny, but that wasn't one of them.

Crowby stole clothespins, my artist mother's paint brushes, our cocker spaniel's bones, cigarettes, and various other objects of interest from around the neighborhood. He stored these treasures on the roof of our turn-of-the century, three-story home.

One of the most amazing things our crow did was to become buddies with our neighbors' miniature Boston terrier, Pogie. The two unlikely friends often played tug-of-war with a stick. What a sight that was! On one occasion they played the game with Pogie's master's underwear, which Crowby had taken from the clothesline.

Our wonderful crow picked up words easily, and he was a natural mimic. He vocalized incessantly, he even called my name. Once a neighbor boy knocked on our door, and Crowby became fascinated with the metal studs on the youngster's jeans. Naturally, Crowby couldn't resist. He pecked and pecked on those bright and shiny toys as the boy yelled, "Help! Help!" repeatedly.

With that, our intelligent black ward had, of course, picked up a new word. Crowby flew through our little town crying, "Help! Help!"

I sometimes wonder what the townsfolk thought of my family's penchant for unusual pets. I like to think they were entertained. They certainly were forgiving, at least. People on the far end of town—a whole mile away!—would call and say, "Crowby is in our back yard. Do you want to come and get him?"

Our charge intimidated salesmen, too. He'd sit on the clothesline or on the tire swing, glaring at them as my father politely conversed with the startled visitors.

When Crowby followed me to school, people were amazed to see a common crow, a wild country bird, flying around the schoolyard and sitting on the window sill outside my or my siblings' classrooms. Those who knew Crowby realized that a crow is no ordinary bird. He made us aware that even the "common old crow" is unique.

Jane Kauzlarich, a native of Hartley, Iowa, grew up surrounded by numerous pets, including dogs, cats, turtles, parakeets, banty chickens, and three pet crows. She's a retired teacher, now living with her husband at the Iowa Great Lakes. She has recently published *Quack*, a children's picture book.

Photo provided by Marti Ritter

JUST WALKING HOME

Marti Ritter

Walking back and forth to country school in the '40s was usually uneventful. Just a few boy-against-girl foot races, a few thrown dirt clods, animals to catch and a culvert or two to explore. When I was in first grade, however, one spring day was the exception.

On that day the air was filled with the sweet smell of fresh-cut alfalfa and lilacs, and a gentle breeze kept us cool as we strolled along. I recall watching my feet and feeling quite special, as I had recently come into possession of my cousin Elsie's shoes. I had never owned such beautiful shoes and this was my first time wearing them. They were Mary Jane-style slippers with a strap that buckled, and they were red. To top off the red shoes, my mother had allowed me to wear my Sunday dress—a red and white checked taffeta. I was a vision, and I knew it.

Our walk to and from school was about a mile with the last quarter of the mile being our driveway. It was always a pleasure to go down the driveway and walk, with a thick grove of trees on either side, before entering the yard and the house.

When we reached the driveway, my brother, Curtis, who was a year ahead of me, decided to run home. He took off like a racehorse. I didn't mind that he left me because the day was beautiful, and I was feeling on top of the world in my Mary Janes.

I meandered along, listening to the swish of my dress, watching my beautiful dressed-up feet. About halfway down the driveway, while still looking at my shoes, I was startled by a movement in the grass alongside the road. Glancing over, I saw a blackish-blue snake slithering slowly along beside me.

Snakes weren't exactly my favorite creatures but I didn't panic. I remember thinking, *I'll just walk faster and he'll get scared and go away.*

So I picked up speed. To my horror, so did the snake! The faster I walked the faster it slithered. When I realized the snake was actually following me, I panicked and began running full-speed, bawling and screaming for my mom.

The snake zipped along just as fast as I did. Try as I might, I couldn't outrun it. My heart was beating so fast that I was gasping for breath as I raced to cover the ground between where I was and the house that seemed so far away.

My father apparently heard me screaming and came out on the porch to see what the commotion was all about. I saw him watching me and then smiling as I came running into the yard.

Then I realized I had another dilemma. The snake was between me and the porch, where my dad was standing. But my panic turned to desperation and bravery as I jumped over the snake and flew up the steps onto the porch.

By then I was sobbing uncontrollably. My dad picked me up and hugged me as he laughed out loud.

I was extremely insulted that he was laughing when I was so scared. But he gently explained just what kind of a snake I was dealing with. He told me that the snake was called a Blue Racer. He said that Blue Racers follow movement. In the old days horses would bolt and run, just like I had done, when followed by a Blue Racer. It was one of the reasons people put "blinders" on horses. The blinders were pieces of leather that stuck out to block the vision on the side of the horses' eyes. That way the horse wouldn't see a snake even if it was racing right beside it.

Dad's explanation comforted me, because I have no lingering phobia of snakes. However, I did insist that my brother walk with me all the way home after that. It was an idea he wasn't particularly fond of, though he did comply. At least for a time.

Marti (Martha) Ritter taught elementary classes for thirty years. She is retired and living in Brookings, South Dakota.

Photo provided by Betty Hembd Taylor

ADVENTURES OF THE HINDT GIRLS: A SPRING DAY

Wanda L. Dover-Stratman

My siblings and I grew up in a village of about five hundred people in Northwest Iowa. I was the middle daughter. My older sister, Leila, was a year and a half older than I, and Jeanne eleven months and three weeks younger. So, if you do the math, my parents had three daughters within three years. Two brothers came along later, but for a while it was just my sisters and me. Our mother referred to us as her "Three Musketeers." If she saw one of us, she said, she saw the three of us. It made parenting easier.

Jeanne and I were, and still are, the very best of friends. The joined-at-the-hip type of friends. Because Mom used to dress the three of us in similar attire, people often thought Jeanne and I were twins.

Though she was younger, Jeanne started telling me what to do from the day she was born. She was always in charge. And, being a shy, obedient child, I did what I was told to do, even when it was Jeanne who was giving me directions. For some reason Leila never seemed to be around when Jeanne came up with her ideas. She missed out on so much!

I recall many times when Jeanne and I had adventures that landed me in trouble. Like the beautiful spring day when we were about four and five years old. It'd been a rainy, dreary spring, and the three of us girls had just gotten new spring boots. I don't think children get to experience "spring boots" today, but it was always exciting for us when we got them. I remember them so clearly. They were not the winter-type boots that fit snugly on the legs. Spring boots, which were of a lighter material, went over the shoes. They stood tall all by themselves when we weren't wearing them. Mine were blue, Jeanne's were red and, if I remember correctly, Leila's were yellow. What a pretty picture they made, three pairs of shiny new boots lined up in the porch. They stood straight, like soldiers, just waiting for the sun to shine so they could be pulled onto excited little girls' feet and serve their purpose. Oh, how we loved our boots! Many times we used to wear them in the house instead of our shoes.

The first warm, sunny spring day finally arrived. We pulled on our boots and took off for the outside and some fresh air. Little did I know how that beautiful spring day would turn to trouble for Jeanne and me. Mom told us we could play wherever we wanted, except the garden. The garden was off limits to us because it was too soft and muddy. Being the obedient child that I was, that was okay with me.

My sisters and I spent the afternoon sloshing around in puddles and walking around the neighborhood to check out everybody else's puddles. We went the two blocks to Grandma's house to see what was happening there. We were having a great time, and trying very hard not to get our new boots muddy.

Eventually we made our way back home. Leila went inside the house. Jeanne and I weren't quite ready to call it an afternoon, so we started messing around in our own backyard. We arrived at that garden we'd been told to stay away from. We just stood at the edge, looking at all that black dirt. There was a long, 2 x 10-inch board lying across the garden, reaching the far side. Now, I would never have thought about doing anything with that board. But Jeanne had this neat idea that we should pretend we were tightrope walkers and walk across the garden on the board.

Oh goodness, that sounded like such fun! And this is where Jeanne's plot came into action. She said, "You go first."

I looked at her doubtfully. Mom had said not to go near or in the garden. Jeanne reassured me that Mom would never know.

"Really, you want me to do that?" I asked. "It was your idea, Jeanne."

"No," she replied, "you go first. You're older and braver than me."

So, since Jeanne was always in charge and always seemed to know what she was doing, I took the first step. I don't know if I expected something awful to happen, but nothing did. The first step was easy. The board didn't move. I slid over so Jeanne could come on board. She did. Still nothing bad happened. So two little girls began inching their way on the board to the middle of the garden.

We were very good at this tightrope-walking thing, and it was fun! We stood there, dreaming about what our garden would soon look like with all of Mom's beautiful flowers, and how much fun we'd have helping her plant the garden.

In the middle of all of our dreaming, Jeanne had another fantastic idea. "Put your foot in and see how soft the dirt really is," she said.

Oh, my, I didn't know about that. My boots might get dirty and Mom said we weren't even supposed to be there.

"Go ahead, Mom won't know," she kindly told me.

So, since Jeanne always seemed to know what she was doing, I attempted to check out the dirt. But I lost my balance and had to put the other foot down to avoid falling. Jeanne grabbed my coat to keep me from tumbling in, and as she did that she had to step into the dirt too. There we were, two little girls with our new spring boots on, standing in the mud. That was bad enough, but as we stood in the dirt trying to assess our situation, we started sinking.

Oh, no! It was quicksand. We just knew we were doomed.

We started yelling and screaming for our mother. I'm sure the whole neighborhood heard us.

Mom and Leila—you know, the sister who had enough sense to go inside—came running out the back door. Mom took one look at Jeanne and me and put her hands on her hips. "What are you doing in the garden?" she asked.

Jeanne told Mom that I'd decided to try to walk on the board across to the other side.

Wait a minute! That wasn't what happened. Before I had a chance to tell my side of the story, Mom told us to just stand there while she thought of some way to rescue us.

"Help us, Mom," we cried. "It's quicksand!"

She assured us that we would be all right, and went back into the house.

There we stood in the garden, crying, in our new spring boots, waiting for Mom to save us. We both looked down at the beautiful boots we loved so much. They were covered with mud and now the tears that fell from our eyes landed on them too. What a sad sight we were.

Mom returned after what seemed like an eternity. In all reality, it was probably just a few minutes. She was wearing her own spring boots and she walked out onto the board. She lifted Jeanne out of her boots and set her on the sidewalk. Then she came back and lifted me out of my boots and took me back to the sidewalk. And then Mom did the most awful thing. She left our new spring boots sitting in the mud in the garden!

"Mom! Mom!" we cried. "Our boots are in the mud."

"Well, you put them there after I told you to please not go near the garden," she replied. "Now let's go in the house and get you cleaned up."

And so our wonderful spring afternoon in our pretty, pretty new boots did not turn out so well. For the rest of the day Jeanne and I would look out the window to see our boots sitting straight and tall in the garden. And we cried because they were stuck in the mud, probably forever.

I have no idea how long Mom left our boots out there but I suspect it wasn't very long. Perhaps she left them overnight so we'd learn a lesson. But even overnight seems like forever when you're young.

We survived that adventure and it wasn't long before Jeanne had other ideas. And yes, I did what she told me to do, and again I was the one who always ended up in the most trouble. Bless our mother's heart, she seemed to understand those harmless learning situations and took it all in stride. When we grew up we often laughed, with Mom, about all of our adventures. She said we were just being normal children, exploring the world.

Now, fifty-some years later, I watch my two youngest granddaughters, ages four and five, and I see Jeanne and me all over again. I watch them, smiling, knowing that they're making their own childhood memories.

If I just take a moment to close my eyes and think back once more to when I was a child, I can hear Jeanne say, "Wanda, let's go outside and look for something to do."

And off we'd go, another chapter in the book of life in the making!

Wanda L. Dover-Stratman and her siblings were raised in a northwest Iowa village steeped in family values and traditions. Today she and her husband reside in Sheldon, Iowa, with her two daughters and their families all being within walking distance. When not on the road working as a tour director for Dover Tours, she enjoys reading, gardening, travel, playing cards and playing the piano.

Photo provided by **Betty** Hembd Taylor

DUCK POND TALES

Dee Kramer

The three of us—my two older brothers and I—took over the Iowa farm on those hot and windy summer days. Shouting and waving, we climbed trees and buildings, rode our bikes and our horse, Topsy. We chased our dog Sandy, and played with the family of cats that roamed our farm. We skated on our short sidewalks and jumped from a ladder onto the sack swing that hung from a tall maple tree near the duck pond. We had lots of places to play: the barn with its inviting hayloft, the empty corncrib, the two-car garage which contained hammers, nails and spare wood, the milk house with cream cans, pails and cream separator, the chicken coop, and the silo. Occasionally, dad would let us use the straw stack next to the barn for a giant slide. Dreaming up new ways to entertain ourselves was the highest priority of each day.

Besides cows, pigs, and two geese, our farm was home to a flock of ducks. To make life more fun for the ducks, Dad had constructed a small concrete duck pond in the grove north of our house. The ducks swam and fluttered around in the pond, but eventually the concrete developed a crack, causing the water to drain. The duck pond remained dry during the summer of 1948.

Our neighbor Adrian and my brothers and I decided to build a ramp leading up to the duck pond and jump it. We were imitating Adrian's hero, Jimmie Lynch of the famous Jimmie Lynch Daredevils. My brothers, both towheads and wiry boys, were energetic and ready for the challenge. They talked excitedly about the jump. Don, age ten, made decisions quickly, and immediately began the project. Verne, age twelve and more thoughtful, decided we needed a good plan. Adrian, a tall, thin boy a few years older, was our project manager. We could always count on him for excellent advice and common-sense problem solving. As the little sister, I was merely allowed to help.

Detailed planning by the boys went into constructing the ramp and calculating the exact upward slope that would be needed to clear the six-foot span with our bikes. Adrian was smart and able to figure things out for us. A long runway in the matted grass was cleared of twigs and debris.

Because Adrian was the oldest of our little group and Jimmie Lynch was his personal hero, we decided that Adrian would be the first to take the daredevil ride.

He started far enough back in the grove, we thought, to get up his speed. He pedaled his bike furiously over the soft, grassy surface toward the ramp.

We cheered him on, "Faster, Adrian, faster!"

Though the ramp held, Adrian didn't have the momentum to clear the six-foot gap over the pond, or perhaps the ramp angle was figured wrong. We watched in horror as the front bike tire hit the far side of the concrete.

Adrian, alias Jimmie Lynch, and the bike landed all tangled together with a thud. We ran to where Adrian lay on the ground.

After a quick assessment, we decided we needed adult help. Adrian, always a quiet boy anyway, didn't speak. He whimpered, his dark eyes staring out from his ashen face. His overalls were torn and his arms were smudged with dirt.

I raced to the house to get Mother and our sister Kathleen.

Mother and Kathleen, abandoning their work in the kitchen, tore out of the house behind me. The screen door banged. Kathleen, a slim teen dressed in blue pedal-pushers and a red blouse, and Mother in a colorful flowered dress with the ever-present apron around her waist, hurried down the gentle slope to the grove.

Adrian was still silent, still lying on the ground. Mother made an evaluation that though Adrian was badly bruised and shaken, it appeared his bones were all intact and he could be transported home.

Kathleen backed our gray 1940 Plymouth close to the accident scene. Then we all gently cradled Adrian in our arms and loaded him into the back seat of the car and the mangled bike into the trunk for the half-mile ride.

My brothers and I stood by the duck pond and watched the gray car with Kathleen at the wheel move down the driveway. Adrian was stretched out on the back seat. Kathleen drove slowly so as not to jostle him. The trunk stood halfway open making our Plymouth look like an old tomcat with an attitude, until the car finally picked up speed on the gravel road as they headed toward Adrian's farm. We heard Kathleen shift from first gear into second gear and then into third gear. A cloud of dust trailed behind the gray Plymouth and settled on the cornfields.

After glasses of Kool-Aid and cookies, my brothers and I spent a few hours clearing away the ramp and trying to decide on some new creative way to fill the rest of a long afternoon.

Just as we were challenging each other to a tree-climbing contest, Adrian walked up our driveway. He was back for more summer fun.

Dee Kramer and her husband Henry live in Orange City, Iowa, and have three children and six grandchildren. Dee worked as a Media Specialist for more than twenty-five years. Her hobbies include traveling, bicycling, photography, art and reading. She conducts trolley tours during the annual Tulip Festival.

Photo provided by Karen J. Schutt

THE BIG PROJECT

Karen J. Schutt

When we were growing up, the grove on our farm was by far our favorite place to play. It was shady under the rows of mature elm, maple, and box elder trees. They grew across the north side and down the west side of the building site, so close together that little sunlight filtered through. This prevented weeds and grass from getting a good foothold and kept the ground under the matted leaves cool and moist to our bare feet. At the far end, away from the road, was a wonderful junk pile of accumulated household trash, rusty old machinery, parts and pieces of this and that discarded by the several families who'd previously lived on the farm. The junk pile provided a wealth of material for our endless projects. It's a miracle none of us ever broke a bone, lost a finger or toe, or required stitches from climbing around on it.

After a family vacation to Yellowstone National Park, my sister Marilyn and I decided to build an oil refinery like the ones we had seen in Wyoming. We used barrels, paint pails, discarded exhaust pipes, buckled eaves troughs, pieces of rusty stovepipe and anything else that we thought would make it look like the real thing. To us it *did* look like the real thing.

On other occasions we built teepees, tree houses, hospitals, grocery stores, a sailing ship, and a candy shop. The candy shop was my favorite creation, and featured "candy corn," "rock candy" and various confections made from "chocolate."

Once we built our own version of an amusement park just like Arnolds Park at Lake Okoboji. That took several weeks to build and was spread out among the trees. We rolled each other around the grove in our Barrel-O-Fun, had a fortune-telling booth, even candy and souvenir shops. The buckled eaves troughs became an elaborate roller coaster. It was a wonderful creation that impressed even the neighbor kids.

One summer day Marilyn decided on a project that would really make people sit up and take notice, but she would need my help. It was to be our biggest project yet. The plan was to dig a lake. Marilyn had seen a goldfish pond in the next town over, and had not forgotten it. But our lake would be much bigger!

We chose a spot among the trees that would give us plenty of room. From the junk pile we found pieces of iron and a broken grain scoop to use for excavating. From the machine shed we borrowed a spade that we promised ourselves we would return. We scraped leaves and grass off the area and started digging.

It was hard work. We sweated and panted. As we worked we talked about how surprised everyone would be when the lake was finished. We decided to tell no one what we were doing. If anyone cared to ask, we'd just say we were playing in our playhouses. At the end of the first day we'd made good progress. The hole was several feet across and a few inches deep, but it would take many more days of digging to make it as large as our plan. We washed off in the cattle tank before going to the house.

The next day after our chores were done, Marilyn and I hurried out to the grove and resumed the excavation. We talked about a name for our lake. It would need a fancy name, like Hidden Lake, or Mystery Lake. Maybe we could even make a little park next to it, like at Spirit Lake. We had spotted a couple of old car gas tanks that would make great seats. Perhaps we could build a bridge across it. A running board from a junked car would make a perfect bridge. What about a dock? We'd have to think about that. Not quite as much progress was made that day, but still we had the satisfaction of seeing it expand.

On the third day we reminded ourselves that we'd need to carefully watch the little ones so they wouldn't fall into the lake and drown. We also decided that Marilyn's playhouse would be on one side of the lake and mine on the other side so we could holler to each other.

The next day we scaled back the size of the proposed lake and decided this would be our last day of digging. By then it was about six feet across and almost a foot deep. We began to wonder how we would fill it. It turned out there was a simple solution. Marilyn said we'd just wait for it to rain. After the rain had filled the lake we would put fish in it. The only fish we knew of were in Grandpa's cattle tank, and he might let us have one or two big goldfish. It wouldn't hurt to politely ask. We might have to be content with making little boats and rafts to float from side to side. It was easy to imagine the water lapping at the edges of our lake, just like at Spirit Lake. It was exciting to think about.

Every day we eagerly watched the sky for possible rain showers, but the days passed bright and sunny. As we waited, we talked about how we would break the news of the lake to our folks. Marilyn came up with the plan. We would get them to take a stroll through the orchard some evening to look at the green apple crop. Then we would casually mention that we had something in the grove we had been working on and would they like to take a look at it? What a marvelous idea! And wouldn't they be surprised. They probably wouldn't believe we had done all that work by ourselves. We could hardly wait!

Finally the morning came when Dad looked at the sky and decided there would be a thunderstorm before the day was over. The air was heavy and sultry and hot. Marilyn and I looked at each other and grinned. Today was the day!

By mid-afternoon we heard thunder in the distance. Gusts of wind bent the trees. Dust devils whirled across the yard, almost upsetting the chickens. Thick gray clouds rose higher in the western sky. The storm was coming nearer.

We raced around the house slamming windows, shooing the chickens into the chicken house, putting away our tricycle and wagon, taking diapers off the clothesline. And then it started to rain.

The rest of the afternoon rain came down in torrents, accompanied by blinding lightning and crashing thunder. At dusk the storm passed, the windows were opened, everything was fresh and clean. A faint rainbow showed briefly in the east before the sun set.

We were so full of anticipation, so excited about how great our lake would surely be, that sleep didn't come easily to us that night.

The next morning Marilyn and I wasted no time getting into our clothes and racing out the door to see our marvelous lake. We slipped and slid around the chicken house, through the orchard and out to the grove.

Marilyn arrived at the lake first. She stopped dead in her tracks. I wasn't far behind. We both stared at our lake. After all our hard work and planning, all the digging and sweating, there was nothing to be seen but a big, muddy hole. There was no water in it at all. We couldn't believe our eyes. What had we done wrong? We had worked so hard. There was no place for fish, no need to watch the little ones, no bridge, no park, no water lapping at the shore, no place to float boats. We looked at each other. I felt like crying. We turned around and trudged slowly back to the house. After a brief discussion, we decided we wouldn't tell anyone about our awful failure, our dream that wasn't to be.

We didn't spend much time in the grove for the next few days. We were still suffering from our loss. After we pushed most of the dirt back into the hole we returned the spade to the machine shed. The hay crop was being harvested so that kept us occupied for several days. Eventually, however, the lure of the junk pile and grove was too much and once again we were hunting for possibilities.

This time I had an idea. A rusty horse-drawn cultivator, with the seat still on and half-buried in the dirt, would make a great airplane. All it needed were some wings. In the junk pile we found some bent windmill blades that would work just fine. After we tied them securely onto the iron wheels with binder twine, the plane was done. And it really could fly!

Karen J. Schutt lives in Sioux Falls, South Dakota, with her husband, Charles. She is a retired teacher, mother of three, grandmother of four, and makes quilts for them all. She believes every child should grow up with a grove and junk pile close by.

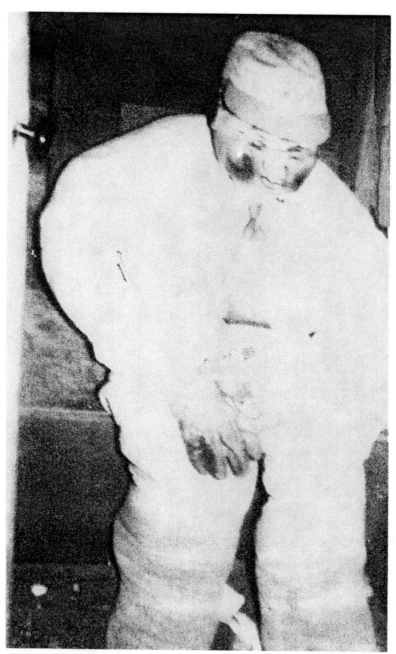

Photo provided by Carolyn Camoriano

OUTHOUSE OSCAR

Carolyn Camoriano

Whenever I come across a dilapidated outhouse on my country road excursions, I think of "Outhouse Oscar" and his escapades in the early 1950s.

Outhouses were a common accessory to many farmhouses and cabins, including our cottage near the small town of Lake View, Iowa. Oscar not only frightened the cottagers, but embarrassed them. My friends and I eventually became his victims.

It all started one afternoon when a retired teacher, Cap Greteman, who spent her summers at a lake cabin near ours, returned from a fishing trip with her brother-in-law, Joe, and her friend, Mary. Cap and Mary docked the boat and went into Cap's cabin, while Joe hurried to the outhouse behind it. Joe started to open the door, but jumped back. Someone was inside! Joe's glimpse showed a large man wearing work clothes and a sport cap, apparently smoking a cigarette and holding a whiskey bottle. "Excuse me," said Joe, and politely stood outside. However, the visitor did not answer.

After what seemed a long wait, Joe said, "Excuse me" louder, and peered in to see if the man had heard him. He then ran next door to report someone in the outhouse. Did the neighbors know who it could be? They didn't know, and didn't care to find out.

The next morning the intruder was gone.

Oscar was discovered a few days later inside the cabin next door, where he was seen from the outside window, relaxing in the living room chair. When the owner saw Oscar, he ran to his car, drove to town and telephoned his wife that there was a tramp in the cottage. Then he found someone to return to the cabin with him. But the tramp had vanished.

Oscar continued to scare the residents that summer. Mrs. Martindale had come to the cottage with her mother. She unlocked the cottage as usual, then walked across the road to unlock the outhouse.

Suddenly she screamed so loudly that all the nearby cottagers ran out to see what had happened. "There's a tramp in there! I think he's dead. I must have locked him in when I left last fall!" When she later returned to the outhouse to check on him, Oscar had disappeared.

Despite the excitement Oscar generated, no rumor of his pranks had reached the four of us college girls, who had arrived to spend a week in my folks' cabin next door.

One evening we walked several miles from town to the cabin after a late movie. The night was dark and quiet. We unlocked the cottage while Joan, the bravest, headed for the outhouse. Suddenly she shrieked and raced to the door, stumbling as her jeans slipped to her ankles. Joan threw herself onto the sofa, shaking and crying. She was unable to talk.

Finally she whispered, "I sat on him!"

"Who?" we asked.

"There's a man in there, and I sat on him!"

There was no phone in the cabin and no way to get help. Finally, Phyllis and Harriett volunteered to check the outhouse with a flashlight. They sneaked close to the little wooden house and flashed a light into it. Then they realized it had all been a joke. Outhouse Oscar was merely a stuffed dummy!

The perpetrator of the Outhouse Oscar hoax was our neighbor, Dean Paulson. As he confessed years later, he'd spent many hours stuffing Oscar with excelsior and putting on his disguise. Sneaking Oscar into outhouses or cabins took much caution. When night came and the neighbors were gone or asleep, Mr. Paulson would stealthily creep out of his cabin, lugging Oscar with him.

After propping him in the outhouses, he waited for the "victims" to appear, chuckling at the hysterical reactions when Oscar was discovered. Making him disappear was even more difficult, but he was usually able to remove the body without being seen.

My former college friends and I are now grandmothers, and our lakeside cabin has inside plumbing. We often tell our grandchildren about the night when Oscar was an uninvited summer guest.

Carolyn Camoriano of Kansas City, Missouri, is a native Iowan. The lake cabin has been in her family since 1911. She and her husband, Julio, have four grown sons and ten grandchildren. She is a freelance writer and poet.

Photo provided by **Ann Johnson**

WE CALL OURS GIDEON

Ann Johnson

Stories of mysterious incidents told by my mother's side of the family for at least sixty years, and who knows how many years before, led to the ultimate conclusion—we have a ghost. An eerie but friendly family ghost, given the name of Gideon.

Creaking floors, doors opening for no reason, and the general feeling of a presence when no one was visible, these events all haunted my maternal grandmother. At first she thought perhaps it was just her active imagination. Until, that is, her daughter, my Aunt Mary, and family moved in to live with Grandma and Grandpa for a while. When others also witnessed such happenings, Grandma realized that she had not been dreaming after all, and they all came to the conclusion that they were indeed living with a ghost.

No one knows *whose* ghost it was, but as you will see, it was a helpful one.

Late one night shortly after they'd moved in, Aunt Mary heard her baby son, Bill, wake up crying. Mary was too tired to get up and rock the fussing baby, though she knew it was the best way to get him back to sleep. She lay there thinking about it, when she heard the rocking chair in the next room start to creak. In short order the baby settled down, and once again there was peaceful silence.

Aunt Mary gratefully assumed that Grandma had gotten up, gone into the next room, and rocked baby Bill back to sleep because she knew how tired Mary was.

The next morning Aunt Mary thanked Grandma for getting up in the night and rocking the baby.

Grandma answered, "I didn't do that."

Hmmm. . . neither had anyone else. Then who had rocked the baby? Who else could it have been? Yes, they decided—Gideon.

During another evening on the farm, all of the men had gone to town to watch a ball game. Grandma and Aunt Mary were home with baby Bill, and Mary's other child, Kitty, age two. Kitty was upstairs in bed, supposedly alone. But when Mary heard her older child giggling and talking, she went upstairs to quiet her. As Mary entered the room, Kitty told her gaily, "Daddy was here! Daddy was here!" The room reeked of cigar smoke. In the family, only Cleo, Kitty's father, smoked cigars. But Cleo was in town with the men and when he returned later and was questioned, denied having been there that night.

Who *had* visited? You guessed it—Gideon!

Kitty seemed to have a special connection to Gideon. Years later she recalled a very vivid memory of "flying downstairs" many times while in that house. She would sit at the top of the stairs, she said, listening to what was going on downstairs, when she would suddenly find herself at the bottom of the stairs. She had no memory of having walked down on her own. It happened a number of times. Even today Kitty says she's never quite figured it out, though she's thought about it often. Her gut feeling is that Gideon carried her down the stairs.

Time passed, and there was yet another incident. This time Grandma was home alone. Grandpa was in town with everyone else from the house and they were expected to be home quite late. Grandma heard the back screen door open, and the sound of footsteps on the floor. She thought it odd, as she was sure she'd hooked the latch. Then she heard the footsteps again, and the door slam shut. Hurrying to the porch, Grandma found no one there. The door was latched shut with the hook on the inside, as usual.

Grandpa and the family arrived home later in the evening, as expected. Grandma asked them about it, but none of them had come home early or gone in the door and out again.

The next morning a man's dead body was found on the roadside across from the farm house. There was no clue as to who he was or even how he died. The family didn't know if the two incidents—the footsteps Grandma heard and the dead man—were connected, but speculation ran high. Did Gideon kill the man who'd been trying to get into the house to perhaps rob or hurt Grandma? Had Gideon opened and closed the back door and had the footsteps belonged to him? Had he been trying to protect "his family"?

Within the family, we believe Gideon lived in the attic of Grandma's house near Peterson, Iowa. The day my own mother and father were married, the reception was held at the farmhouse. That very evening the house burned to the ground. We've had no traces of Gideon since, even after the house was rebuilt.

Kitty, who recounted stories of "flying" down the stairs in the old house, had no further experiences of that kind.

Perhaps the friendly ghost chose this way and time to depart, or perhaps the fire scared him off. Or who knows, it may have been his rebellion against my mother's marriage. You never can tell with ghosts.

It's been fifty-four years since we've heard from Gideon. All we have left are some unusual stories and fond memories of "our family ghost" and one tattered picture of Grandma's house on a snowy night.

If you look closely you can spot the outline of a man, top hat and long coat, watching from the shadows.

That's Gideon.

Ann Johnson moved to the Iowa Great Lakes area with her two daughters from Osage, Iowa, in 1988. She met Wayne Johnson in 1999 and they married in 2002, creating a family of three daughters and one son, along with seven grandchildren for the couple. Ann passed away on October 1, 2009, just days before this book went to print.

1956 - 2009

Photo provided by Ralph Scherder

THE ZIPPER

Ralph Scherder

The fair came to our town every June and ran for five days. Many people can't stomach fair rides—too many circles, compared to the roller coasters found at amusement parks. But I loved them. It takes a certain appreciation to love fair rides, to actually *want* to go around in circles.

As a kid, I could ride the Gravitron twelve times straight, grabbing a handful of peanuts and a swig of lemonade between spins. The Gravitron was a spaceship-looking beast of flashing lights on the outside and neon darkness within. You stood against a padded wall, and as it began to spin like a top you'd feel gravity pushing you up the wall. You felt pressures inside, too, things shifting around in there that shouldn't be shifting. Older people getting off the ride often ran for the bathroom.

Every fair or carnival has one ride meant to strike fear in a rider's heart. At our town's fair, that was the Zipper. Its name alone was like a pterodactyl's talon across soft underbelly. The Zipper looked prehistoric, a great yellow machine with oddly shaped, free-spinning yellow cages on a vertical oval track. Being top-heavy, they spun headlong into space, then would rock backwards halfway, and again plunge forward a full turn.

On two occasions I rode the Zipper only to hear a groan from the cage above me and someone saying, "I think I'm going to be sick," just moments before the premonition came true. The outer covering of the cages was made of wire mesh, which filtered out the big chunks.

When the ride stopped and the woozy evacuated, a carnie stood armed with a garden hose.

The first time I rode the Zipper was with my grandma. Seeing her get on the ride boosted the confidence of many middle-aged men waiting in line. After all, my grandma, bogged down by arthritis, could barely walk without hobbling. But the weak appearance was deceptive. Beneath it beat the heart of a lioness.

As my grandma often said, she grew up on Tough Street. The farther down the street you went, the tougher they got. She'd lived in the last house.

Doctors had predicted arthritis would make Grandma wheelchair bound by the time she was thirty. But here she was, limping up the ramp to take me on the Zipper. My grandma—tough, but if you hugged her too hard you could hear her back crack in a half dozen places. Once we were in the cage, she made sure the bar was tight across our laps, and her gnarled hands gripped the cross support. She winked at me. "I'll make it," she said, "if they have to carry my pieces out in a bucket full of vomit."

She lived, and walked off the ride in one piece, giving more men in line false confidence and resulting in more cages later being hosed down.

Grandma and I enjoyed a stretch of about three years riding the Zipper together. Finally the abuse became too much for her joints, so she set about finding riding partners for me. Her searches were always successful. She'd tell me to wait by the Zipper while she walked off into the crowd with her bag of cotton candy and some fresh-squeezed lemonade. Without fail, she'd return with a female riding partner, a girl my age.

I didn't know what to say to any of these girls. I was shy and awkward, and it was a challenge to hold their attention long enough to keep them from jumping line. I could've ridden by myself, I guess, but to me the fair was a place for friends and couples. I felt especially alone when standing in a line where everyone else had a partner.

Grandma reeled them in and I kept riding. One day I rode the Zipper eight times in a row, and each time, as I got off, Grandma had another girl waiting. Which couldn't have been an easy feat. With red hair and more freckles than Opie Taylor, I was cute in the way ugly dogs are cute. The sun intensified my complexion by turning my face, arms, and legs into one giant freckle.

The best of Grandma's girls stood four and a half feet tall and wore a white blouse, blue slacks, and had cropped brown hair. She was tomboyish, so plain she was beautiful, a girl who wouldn't be afraid to roll up her pant legs, wade creeks, and turn over rocks to find crayfish.

Her name was Heather and she was at the fair with her grandfather, who was over by the Tilt-A-Whirl, offering a box of popcorn to my grandma. Heather said she hoped the line for the Zipper moved quickly, as she was playing saxophone in the band that performed between tractor pulls. She thought that growling noise moving the air was the tractors starting up. She worried that she'd soon hear the announcement over the loudspeakers for all band members to check in.

The line moved forward. Two spins of the Zipper later, it was our turn to get on. We'd been standing side-by-side for nearly ten minutes, but that still hadn't prepared me for when we got on that ride together. In the cage we were pressed so close that I could smell her. She was too young for perfume, but she smelled sweet, smelled of something that takes a while to fix into your olfactory, but once it's there it hangs around a long time. I felt dizzy before the ride even started.

Every ride at the fair had its own sound system and played its own type of music. For slower rides, like the Ferris wheel, the music was usually soft rock. For high-energy rides like the Zipper it was full-scale, guitar-screaming rock-and-roll, and at that particular time Poison had peaked on the Billboard charts. The ride operator must've been a huge Poison fan. One Poison tune after another blasted so loudly that their music has become a permanent part of my memory. The two structures, music and memory, have merged so completely that even today when I hear a Poison song I smell sweet, little-girl skin and remember the feel of Heather next to me.

Heather was the only riding partner I ever had who asked me questions. She wanted to know about me, which caught me off guard. I could think of nothing to say that would make me seem less dull. I was a simple kid. I liked baseball, books, and going on rides that went upside down. I didn't know what to say to a pretty girl.

Suddenly our cage lurched into motion. We rocked backward as we ascended, facing up into the evening sky. At that moment I felt anything was possible.

Strange things happened inside me as the cage reversed field. My guts went forward as my body went back. The narrow gap between Heather and me vanished as we were pushed to one side of the seat. She leaned into me hard, our skin touching from

169

our arms to our legs. A weak feeling came up in me as the popcorn and lemonade I'd consumed before the ride churned in my stomach. I thought: "I can't do it, she's got a white blouse and she's playing sax between truck pulls."

When Heather apologized and inched away, the feeling passed. It returned when she was again propelled into me. It was the strangest sick feeling I'd ever had. Except it wasn't sick at all, but a warmth. It intensified when she didn't move away this time, instead linking her arm through mine.

Then, during the greatest moment of my life, came that prophetic groan from the cage above us: "I'm going to be. . ."

It splattered against the mesh. Brown, raindrop-sized blotches stained Heather's blouse. She buried her face in my shoulder and her body trembled beside mine. I thought she was crying until she threw back her head and howled with laughter. We spun and rocked and screamed and held on, and I tried to say, "The stains aren't too bad, you can hardly tell," when a big chunk centered a hole in the mesh and passed through untouched. It pelted Heather's slacks and ricocheted off my tennis shoes. A quarter section of hot dog. But not just any old Oscar Meyer wiener. This puppy was a beef dog, extra thick, and it rattled around by our feet before falling through a gap in the floor.

The ride slowed. Our cage leaned forward, forward, seemed to teeter, and we leaned into it to make it spin one more time around. We sat there, no gap between us, smiling. So high. Looking off in different directions. To the hazy south, the fishing boats on the lake looked like bugs on glass.

"Thank you for riding with me," Heather said.

"Any time," I said.

Her gaze shifted westward. "Sometimes it feels great just to scream your lungs out."

There were so many things I wanted to ask her. What made it so good to scream? There were many things I wanted to know, but I was so dumb. So dumb and shy.

The ride brought us, in increments, closer to the ground. As we waited for the inevitable I had that feeling of not wanting to get off, not being ready for it to end quite yet. Like there had to be a better ending than merely stepping off the ride.

Heather turned to me abruptly and said, "I'm going to the junior high this fall."

I said, "Me too."

"Orientation's coming up. We could go together."

"Sure."

"If you don't want to. . ." She looked away.

"I want to." I placed my hand over hers. "Really."

The Zipper moved. Our cage rocked backward, giving us one more thrill before we touched ground.

My grandma watched approvingly as Heather scribbled her phone number on a torn-off piece of her grandfather's empty popcorn box.

Already, before we even said good-bye and she ran off to get her instrument, I knew I wouldn't call her. I tucked the phone number in my pocket. When I pulled it out later, I'd tell myself that her handwriting was illegible. The two could be a three, the five a six, and some of the numbers too grease-smeared to read. Grandma would ask if I'd ever called and I'd say, "No," and she'd say, "You're just like your pap. If I hadn't hog-tied him and dragged him to the altar, he'd still be a happy man." She'd say, "You know what your problem is? You're afraid of rejection."

Except I wasn't afraid of rejection. I'd heard, a year earlier, that some magazines paid hundreds of dollars for stories, and I'd been receiving rejections from them ever since. So I was used to rejection.

I certainly wasn't afraid Heather would want too much too soon – marriage, kids, a big house. It wasn't that. We were only twelve, after all.

I feared the expectation that comes with a relationship. It was easier to have a single, perfect moment and always wonder "what if?" than to taint the memory with something never quite fulfilling. You can get a lifetime of joy from a single moment.

School started that fall and Heather wasn't there. I asked around. She'd moved away. Her mother had died of brain cancer and she was now living in Nevada with her dad.

After finding that out, I regretted not calling her. Over the next fifteen years I often wondered what'd become of her. Summers crept up and Junes settled in. The fair changed some. The rides mostly, in the way they looked. Even the Gravitron got a makeover to a more realistic-looking UFO. Not that it matters. I don't have the stomach for those rides anymore.

The Zipper was removed a few years ago. One of the cages broke off the track and cart-wheeled nearly fifty feet before slamming into the Tilt-A Whirl. Fortunately it happened early in the morning, before the fair was open, during a practice run. They've replaced the Zipper with a ride that doesn't even come close to going upside down.

The tractor pulls are still popular. In fact, the night those take place is the busiest night of the whole fair. Every couple of years I climb the grandstand and look back over the rides and wonder if some boy is having the greatest night of his life.

Mostly, though, I think about myself. And Heather. In my mind I see us, two kids on the Zipper. The moment was every-thing, and going in circles never felt so good.

Ralph Scherder lives in Herman, Pennsylvania, and is the author of *The Taxidermist's Son*. His short stories have appeared in *North Dakota Quarterly, The Literary Review, The Iconoclast,* and many others.

Photograph by Dan Ruf

THE CANVAS OF RURAL AMERICA

Dan Ruf

There's a golden sunrise outside my living room window and the remnants of a passing storm can be heard in the distant thunder. The air smells fresh from the rain and the earth is cleansed. Spears of golden light weave their way through the disappearing cloud masses, their edges highlighted by heaven's gold. On almost any morning in Iowa the rising sun becomes a spiritual awakening for me. Nature's pallet of colors is laid open for all to see and marvel. And as the sun rises higher the cross-cut shadows give form to the land beneath it.

The air is cool and the gravel road is calling to me, while the wild flowers call to my camera. The spring flush of floral brilliance gives way to nature's summer garments. Birds-foot trefoil with its bright yellow flower is beginning to burst from the ground and wild roses are in full bloom. A doe spies me from her hiding place and her fawn skitters back into the dense foliage. Nature is well. I feel complete in it.

Farther ahead a mallard drake and hen splash upward from the Little Ocheyedan River. The golden ripples reflecting the quieting sunrise spread their light up the river. The high-pitched call of the killdeer can be heard and I spot her clutch of small cotton balls on stilts running behind her. The quietness of this land, at this hour, is unforgettable and probably is the reason I like to stroll down these gravel byways.

I would defy city folk to come to this quiet corner of the world and not feel the relaxing solitude. They will be overcome by the lushness of nature's carpet and her symphony of sounds. The peepers maintain a continuous whistle that can give calm to the ragged heart. The brown thrush repeats its repertoire of songs to any passing ear. This is a peaceful world, a place for quiet contemplation.

As the morning rolls along I find myself in May City, a town that may be gasping its last breath. The May City Store sits on the north side of the street and was once referred to jokingly as the May City Mall. Joyce and Bill Shattuck were the proprietors of the store for years.

Joyce had a smile that was as happy as her soul. She was keeper of the announcement board that told of local birthdays and anniversaries. Chairs sat in a row within easy reach of Joyce's pastries and coffee, and many mornings I stopped to take my break in one of those seats. Bill was a great storyteller and a gadget man. If someone didn't know how to fix something, chances are Bill did. To a city kid like myself, listening to Bill speak of the days of farming in years past was comforting. When Bill passed, Joyce later sold the store and it was never the same. I miss the warmth of that rural rest stop.

Across the street is Curt's Repair. Whatever a person has that's broken, Curt can fix. He's a hardy man with a good heart. His long hair and beard disguise the comedic soul that resides within, but his reputation is in the strength of what he crafts. I once chided him about the fact that he made everything so much better and heavier than it was before. With a quick wit and smile he shot back that he never knew what a farmer might do with it.

The shop is the heartbeat of this town, as it has always been, a gathering place for farmers and their sickly implements. This is a news library where just about everything is fodder for discussion. Grain prices, steel prices, crop conditions, snowfall or a sick friend are all issues on the daily agenda. If you've been a long time in the field, a few minutes at Curt's will catch you up to date on the county happenings.

A few years ago Curt got fed up with the daily grind of his business and quit it for a day job with the rural water company in town. We farmers mourned our loss and Curt must have seen the error of his ways because he came back to his shop . . . our shop.

Many old friends have passed from this town, but their memories live on. Young kids who once raided the candy counter at the store while waiting for the school bus are now adults with families and farm chores. When I see them I'm reminded of what a good crop of workers our rural family has raised. Some have moved away for better jobs, but they return to get revitalized by the rural time clock. They too recall their childhood history with their children, the stories of the hayloft, the fishing hole and the county fairs. The town's history passes to another generation in word, but will not be lived again. Our rural life is changing and dwindling with time, and in time will not be heard from again, at least not in its present form or state of being.

But the land is here to be a part of our souls. The changing seasons, the harshest winters and the hottest summers are balanced by the refreshing spring days and the long, crisp fall mornings. If we wander this land during its passage of time we still see the migrating geese and the new year's fawns. We hear the wind as it passes through the tall grass prairies that cling to their place in this land. The rooster ring-necked pheasants still strut along the roadside and add their colorful place in the sunrise pallet of colors.

Every bend in the river waits for us to sit down and listen to its lulling harmony, its whisper of life. We can linger here and let it refresh the spirit. We can open memory's book and recall our childhood days spent at the water's playground. But as we age we sense the full harmony that the flowing waters leave with us.

The passage of time may change the land, but it will not change the land's impression on us if we allow its peace to come into our lives. We have to step foot into this arena, open the car door and actually step out onto the rich earth for its peace to flow through us. We must open every sense of our being for the harmony of this rich earth to fill us, and when we abandon all our prejudices we will begin to understand the importance of the preservation of this precious land. It will no longer be just a provider to us as farmers and ranchers. It will, as the Creator, rouse our spirit, touch our lives and fill our being with its calm simplicity.

And the canvas of rural America will once again be prepared and waiting for the peaceful colors that we place upon it. It will respond to each brush stoke of our lives and reveal our living history within its borders. And the colors that we splash on this canvas will make a record and possibly be the masterpiece of our lives on this earth. And when the last stroke has been swept across the ever-changing canvas of life it will stand as the heritage that we pass on to our children. It will be our living history and timeline that will tell the story of our lives and will be a legacy of our footprint in this world. . . on this land.

Dan Ruf is a retired northwest Iowa farmer, serving his other two passions of photography and writing from his home in Spirit Lake, Iowa.

Photo provided by Karen J. Schutt

ORDER FORM

Mail order form to: Shapato Publishing
PO Box 476
Everly, IA 51301

Please send _____ copies of

Knee High by the Fourth of July:
More Stories of Growing Up
in and Around Small Towns in the Midwest

at $14.00

+ .98 sales tax each

S&H per quantity:

$3.00 for 1 – 3 copies

Enclosed is check or money order for:

$_____ Payable to Shapato Publishing.

NAME:

ADDRESS:

Or order safely online at:

www.ShapatoPublishing.com

LaVergne, TN USA
14 December 2009
167027LV00004B/155/P